I0542919

SEVEN LETTERS

"Now I saw heaven opened and behold a white horse. And He who sat on him was called Faithful and True, and in righteousness He and makes war."

—Revelation 19:11

www.greggb4hope.com

SECOND EDITION

SEVEN LETTERS

DETAILING THE PROPHETIC FRAMEWORK
OF THE RETURN OF CHRIST

GREGORY A. BOOKER

PROMINENT
BOOKS

5830 E 2nd St, Ste 7000 #9983
Casper, WY 82609
USA

CONTENTS

A SPECIAL THANKS

To ALL THOSE WHO ENCOURAGED me to continue by lending me their ear and their time, their talent, and their hope in Christ—Pastor Hanserd, Michael, Frank, Carla, Ron, Ethan, Morris, Sharon, John, Dennis, Vicki, Pastor Cooper, and countless others whom the Lord has brought before me. And last, but not least, the voice of the Spirit.

This second edition is a combination of two separate books into one book. The previous books were titled *Seven Letters Detailing the Prophetic Framework of the Return of Christ* and *Inspired Writings of a Prophet for Jesus the Christ*. They are edited and merged to benefit the readers with better pricing and to give a more complete view of the author's vision, experience, and mission.

> "And it shall come to pass in the last days, saith God, I will pour out of my Spirit upon all flesh: and your sons and your daughters shall prophesy, and your young men shall see visions, and your old men shall dream dreams: And on my servants and on my handmaidens I will pour out in those days of my Spirit; and they shall prophesy" (Acts 2:17–18).

SUMMARY OF SCRIPTURE USED IN THE SEVEN LETTERS

THE KEY SUPPORTING SCRIPTURES USED throughout this book and the corresponding letters include:

LETTERS 1-3
- Matthew 24—"When is the sign of thy coming and the end of the world?"
- Daniel 9:22–27—The seventy weeks which are upon Israel and the Holy City.
- Romans 11—The Olive Tree Parable: The covenant of forewarning to Christians and the covenant of hope for Israel.

LETTER 4
- Daniel 2, 7, 8, 11, and 12—The Ten-Horned Kingdom; the personality of the Antichrist; the stone that smote, and an everlasting kingdom!
- Revelation 13:1–8—Ten horns supported by seven heads

LETTER 5

- John 21:15–25—Who is "another" to follow Peter as Peter would not?
- Revelation 17—Mystery Babylon points a finger at Rome!

LETTER 6

- Romans 11—This is my covenant I make with them! What Christians should know about "the other covenant"!
- 1 Corinthians 12–14—Importance of the prophetic ministry
- Revelation—Who are the tribulation saints and why are they?; Old testament prophets and New Testament apostles; prophesy concerning Israel's return as a nation and that the nations shall be tested as Israel was!

LETTER 7

- Genesis 3:14–15 and Romans 5:18–19—The full measure of Jesus Christ
- 1 Thessalonians 5—Shall peace and safety bring sudden destruction and why?; the purpose of the Seventieth Week of Daniel and the Antichrist
- Matthew 24—Jesus answers the questions that the Jews ask; the world is judged by the Messiah at last
- Ezekiel 38–39 and Revelation 19—The battle of Armageddon; the crowning of the faithful amen

PREFACE

EPHESIANS 4:11–13 SAYS, "AND HE gave some, apostles; and some, prophets; and some, evangelists; and some, pastors and teachers; for the perfecting of the saints, for the work of the ministry, for the edifying of the body of Christ: till we all come in the unity of the faith, and of knowledge of the Son of God, unto a perfect man, unto the measure of the stature of the fullness of Christ."

It is, therefore, my good pleasure to introduce to the Church, for the Church, but not necessarily by the Church, a message that I hope and pray might accomplish the objectives of Ephesians 4:11–13.

The following introductory comments I deem critical as they aid in bridging the seven letters together. Though each letter is separate and distinct and can stand alone on its own merit, the central theme of Christ's return is ever present. Also each letter is dated with when it was written—prior to many of the world events that are now occurring. This boldness, the Lord required of me in order to establish credibility working in the office of a prophet.

It is peculiar that the number seven gave me a sense of completion, although I had anticipated writing eight letters. Seven is often known as God's number, and it means completion. Therefore, let us think of this book as a series of seven different frames or pictures as concluding evidence concerning the nearness of Christ's return for His Church.

When all is said and done, my sole purpose of publishing these letters is that we might come into the unity of the faith, culminating into the knowledge of the full measure of Christ. A partial measure will yield only a partial knowledge of Him, and the perfect man we can become will not be manifested without such a full gospel. So it is to the glory of God that such truths should be made known in their fullest at this most appropriate time.

I do claim that these letters were written under inspiration and, as such, become a vision and an experience. The Scripture commands us to try the spirit. Therefore, I request of the churches to challenge me in this regard. These letters are not above nor meant to replace the Bible as so many others have done by producing books and claiming them to be equal to the Bible. However, I do claim that they are firmly built upon biblical examination and, as a result, are supported by Scripture.

I have done nothing but believe by faith in His Word as His Word is written. However, His Word as written is what many in the church have great difficulty accepting. But may it be the will of God that these letters aid us in overcoming this problem.

I do apologize for having such a lengthy title, but try as I did, I could find no shorter solution. Every word of it is critical to grasping the full reality of what is facing not only the churches but also the world. As such, a few comments are in order.

First, the word "detailing" means a very thorough and complete study of the reality of prophecy, considering both the Old and the New Testament, ancient Israel, and the new covenant church. I have detailed certain events which support fulfillment of prophecy related to modern Israel and to the churches, such as "end times...last days...etc." as seen in Scripture.

Second, this book contains information to support what has been revealed to me. Please give it at least one good reading. It is intended to give insight and clarity concerning our generation. I truly want you and your family to consider something that may seem unrealistic but, if given an ear, is very possible and is very true nonetheless.

Third, many events in the world today verify the Word of God and prove that God is not working mysteriously or in secret. It is our lack of study combined with an unbelieving nature that blinds us to the fulfillment of prophecy. I pray that my efforts may be of benefit to you and those around you. The Spirit of Truth tells me that, if it is given to me to know, then by faith it is my responsibility to reveal (Luke 12:48).

The world has experienced a dramatic and eerie change recently with more anticipated changes to occur. Current world politics, economics, agriculture, banking, and even our religious beliefs are being challenged and ultimately affected like never before. Also, racial and ethnic strife appear ready to explode in the USA like it already has in many other places on this planet. The question we must ask ourselves is: If there is a God, how and when will He reveal Himself?

There is a modern phenomenon that "as a nation" has not existed for almost two thousand years. That nation is none other than Israel. Without knowing your beliefs, I ask you to consider Israel and its unique link to the Bible as a sign of the "True God" and as a sign of the second coming of Christ. That nation was once again restored in 1948 and has continuously been in the news for all the world to see. It is as if that nation is a thorn in the Earth's side. Think about it...think about it...and then think about it again.

Yes, all true prophecy glorifies the return of the Messiah at the appointed time. Dates are not important, but the signs are. The Bible makes clear what to watch for. Therefore, I have watched and know the signs, and so I forewarn. Knowing that you may not know the many promises for those who believe on His name, let it be said that eternal life is one of them and Israel's restoration after so long of a dispersion is the very evidence of God's eternal existence. Therefore, my brethren, rejoice, but understand that God must deal with those who are in unbelief, and there are many, for such is the price of free will.

Fourth, I proclaim that I have been moved by the Holy Spirit to write what I have come to know for the benefit of others. So I appeal to one and to all to consider these words placed in my heart by the Spirit of Truth. No man knows the day, and I do not intend on giving a day. But let us remember, does not our Lord say "Watch!"? Will not He reward them that look for Him? Are we not commanded to hope? And so it is written in John 3:3—"And every man that hath this hope in [H]im purifieth himself, even as [our Lord] is pure."

I have often asked the question "Why me, Oh Lord? Why am I given such divine insight concerning the mysteries of your Word and am so compelled to reveal them to all?" The Spirit of Truth always gives me one simple answer—the right questions, the ones most are afraid to consider, must be asked! And so I searched and sought out answers for such difficult questions, praying that I would never lose sight of the "correct perspective." For it was already being made clear that by the type of inquiries, I was acknowledging the "correct perspective" of God and God alone.

I have no degree in theology. I have no experience in ministering the Word, and I have only been attending church within the last three years on a regular basis after almost twenty years of absence. However, I became interested in the legitimacy of prophecy, and with a fondness for the history of man, asked two simple questions:

- Question #1—Realizing that the Old Testament dealt almost exclusively with Israel, I asked "What is the meaning of Israel's rebirth in May 1948 and does it have any prophetic significance?"
- Question #2—Without doubting the literal intent of the Book of Revelations, I asked "How could man be so wrong and God be so right that such a book had to be written?"

And so I began a consuming search for truth. Could Islam and Christianity, which disagree with each other, both be right? God forbid! If this were the case, righteousness would have no honor. The True God must speak to all men the same—my absolute principle. However, let us be well aware of the fact that man does have free will, but unfortunately, free will is no guarantee that one is in accordance with God's will.

And so I searched, studying prophecy, Jewish history, and religion in general. I purchased over twenty books, costing a mere $250, and read them in less than eighteen months. (Certainly a small investment but a great revelation.) I found the emphasis of the True God is not religion but truth, for truth is a fact demonstrated by God Himself. That is what I really see when studying Christ's first coming. And I see the truth demonstrating itself slowly but surely against the many false doctrines (a.k.a. religion) of this illustrious generation in preparation of Christ's second coming. Now I see what the great apostle Paul was blessed to see for our benefit by the grace of God, and the Spirit of Truth directs me to write it down. For it is written in Jeremiah 33:3, "Call to me and I will answer you and tell you great and unsearchable things you do not know."

Therefore, I desire that my efforts and my faith by the grace of God add knowledge, insight, clarity, and hope in these most challenging times. There is indeed a light at the end of the tunnel, and that light is none other than Jesus, who the Spirit bares record in 1 John 5:11, "And this is the record, that God hath given to us eternal life, and this life is [only] in [H]is Son."

After a period of saturation in the study of God's Prophetic Word, I experienced a baptism of the Holy Spirit. It was unknown to me at the time what I was going through, but I experienced a calling and a commission by God to write what I have come to know for the benefit of the Church. The desire was surging constantly within me to tell the people. Prophecy, as in days past, is alive and well and moving before our eyes, but the multitude is failing to see what we ought to be able to see. In other words, we see with our eyes but we don't see with our mind. God touched me to reveal the prophetic word as a result of my intense desire to want to know the reality of Him in preparation of Christ's return. This is my first effort at writing, and it came because of a born-again experience. It's real. Read the book in its entirety, and see it in action.

Thank you and amen!!! May what I have to say be acceptable to your heart. Let us begin.

INSPIRED WRITINGS

AND THE HAND OF THE LORD WAS UPON ME
A Baptism by the Spirit

IT HAPPENED ON A DAY in April of 1990, in the living room of my home. I was alone, very alone, that day. I had left work early just to study the Bible and pray. I was seeking for something that I knew was there, and I was continuing my quest to attain a higher understanding of Jesus Christ.

Sitting on the sofa while reading a book titled Sermon on the Mount, I laid my head back, meditating on His Word and, ultimately, His righteousness. Without realizing it, I began to slip into a trance, a very deep trance. I found myself unable to move but being moved nonetheless, for there was a weight upon me that was driving me slowly but surely from the sofa to the floor. I was laid prostrate, and the weight was continuing to press upon my back. Attempting to get up, I could not do so, literally or in the vision. Yes, there was a vision set before me.

As I struggled to get up but could not, at the tilt of my head, I saw a stake set in the rocky ground. Since it appeared to be dusk, all I could see was the base of the stake for there was nothing else to see. Suddenly, I had an eerie and yet profound feeling that someone was hanging on that stake and that someone was me. I remember thinking, *Why am I thinking of me hanging on a stake if I am laid upon the ground?* And this is what puzzled me throughout the whole vision.

I struggled to gaze up at the top of the stake by slowly and with much effort looking upward with my eyes because the weight continued pressing firmly on me. Attempting to stand, I could not! As I raised my head and eyes, I saw the feet and then the knees. The light around me was fading since it was dusk, but I was determined to see the waist and then the torso.

I truly felt that I would see myself hanging on the cross. I felt dead, and yet I was alive. Certainly I anticipated myself hanging on that stake for I also felt my sins in that moment. Yes, the weight of my own sins seemed to condemn me for I knew I was before the Lord.

I continued raising my head, and I saw shoulders, and then I saw the head. The whole body, falling forward, was literally torn and bleeding. I gazed in amazement. Yes, even awe, if you will, and yet I felt utter shame and ultimately fear, but oh, was there also so much joy. For it was not me who was on that cross! It was someone else.

I whispered, "Is that Jesus?"

I knew He had taken my place for it was I who should have been up there, and yet there He was through no fault of His own.

Suddenly, a voice boomed out of the sky, and I found myself standing on my feet. The voice said most profoundly, "This is what my beloved Son has done for you."

Falling to my knees, I cried while thanking my Lord, indeed. The voice was fearsome, but now it was not given unto me to fear for I felt whole, even renewed. I felt baptized by the Spirit of the Lord.

The vision ended, and I opened my eyes, finding myself on the floor instead of the sofa where I had been sitting. I was sweating and had lost all concept of time. Though time seemed short due to the events, I knew that it was not, because the clock approximated at least over an hour had passed.

I asked myself, *Did I have an out-of-the-body experience?* The exact answer I may never know, but this I do know: "I am crucified. Nevertheless, Christ is alive in me." I did thank the Lord for His long-suffering patience toward me and acknowledged before Him that I am at His service.

After the vision, I continued studying the prophetic Word of the Lord, and on May 16, 1990, while at work in my private office, a voice came upon me and said, "Now write what you have come to know." Without hesitation, I wrote my first Prophetic Letter, and so began the work that the Lord has called me to do. And Seven Letters is that work.

THE UPPER ROOM VISIT

ON A COLD WINTER NIGHT in Rockford, Illinois, a group of writers and poets sat around a table reading their various works. The purpose of the meeting was to share our talents and, more importantly, to express our faith in our Lord Jesus. On this particular night, the thought of what this could lead to entered my mind. Here we were down in the lower level of the public library. However, I sensed the Lord was making it His upper room. All of us came from diverse backgrounds and covered all ages and denominations. We were few in number, but new faces continued to show up at the meetings, giving us new insights and always the joys of a believer in Christ. Clearly, something was going on as the Lord continued to draw others to this creative venue in hopes of publishing material with Jesus as our focus.

The Rockford Christian Writer's Guild had a vision to put their faith in Lord Jesus in print. It's an effort to express, share, and promote through the pen *how* the Lord continues to work through those who He touches with His Spirit. I personally have found more joy being in the Lord than *doing* something for Him and, as result, seem to do even more for Jesus. Such is the essence of the collective works of inspired writings that make up this book. It would be easy to let them collect dust on a closet shelf, written but never read. Thoughts that are never spoken! This position I chose not to take, hoping just one unbeliever may be touched to know the Word is our Light, and in it, nothing is hid.

And what is the purpose of these writings? Personally, I want to *restore* the faith and the hope that was set two thousand years ago, with prophecy being the vehicle of delivery as the Spirit giveth. Let us remember that Jesus is the spirit of prophecy, and He is The Prophet of prophets. I simply work in His office. These inspired writings are meant to speak His hope and His forewarning in preparation of a deliverance to come some day. I pray daily that I put forth the prophetic word, being also a part of His ministry, for the glory of God and bringing others to that marvelous light. In 2 Peter 1:19–21 it is written: "We have also a more sure word of prophecy, whereunto ye do well that ye take heed, as unto a light that shineth in a dark place, until the day dawn, and the day star arise in your hearts. Knowing this first, that no prophecy of the Scripture is of any private interpretation. For the prophecy came not in old time by the will of man: but holy men of God spake as they were moved by the Holy Ghost."

Reflecting on the crucifixion of Christ, there were only two men willing to openly take Jesus down from the cross by the time He breathed His last breath on the cross. These men were Joseph and Nicodemus, for the disciples abandoned the cross out of fear for themselves. God always has someone to do His work, so it didn't matter that the disciples were not present. For by the grace of God, Jesus held nothing against them. Jesus showed them a resurrected Savior, they continued to be His disciples, and their hope was restored.

During Jesus's post ministry after His resurrection, the twelve disciples became 120 disciples, waiting for something of which they knew not of. They were directed to wait and to wait together in the upper room, expecting. Then on the day of Pentecost, their faith was rewarded and empowered; they gave birth to the Church, and the world hasn't been the same since. I believe that such a phenomenon—a quest for the righteousness of God in a self-righteous world—is being established now in these perilous times by the Spirit of God. The world is in deep pain as it struggles to live with a God but with disregard for any truths or laws from God. Such was the case in the upper room; those 120 precious believers were being set to restore God's position. They were moved by the Spirit to preach hope through salvation, and the platform was Christ and Christ only. After the passing of approximately two thousand years, could the world be falling back to those times and in need of the reality of God through divine intervention once again on an even a grander scale, if you will?

In my study of God's Word, there is a consistent error made by the people of God throughout biblical history. We fail to ask God what is His plan for Himself? Being too concerned with ourselves all too often, we never seem ready to hear this higher purpose. I have searched Scripture diligently for God's purpose for Himself and have been inspired to write the experience for the benefit of the Church. Let's meet once again in the study room of our mind in preparation of His return because I got the feeling that the Lord is making ready a fresh anointing for the new millennium. Peace be unto you through our Lord, the Christ.

LET THERE BE

In the midst of Change...Let there be Stillness.

In the midst of Disappointment...Let there be Contentment.

In the midst of Confusion...May there be Patience.

Yes! In the hour of our Testing...Always let there be Faith!

And in our moment of Despair...Let there yet be Hope.

Despite being in the midst of these Calamities...Remember that Jesus
Christ can indeed Cope!

Let there be Silence...That we might whisper our Prayers.

Let there be Joy...That we might sing our Songs.

And let there be Peace...That we should wait
on the Lord however long.

Finally, if one thing we must let there be...Let there be Love
that it might be among us All.

For without such Love in our hearts might we Fall.

So as we grow, we may yet shed a few more Tears,
seeking a more perfect Kingdom.

Nevertheless, let us come Near.

Therefore, I pray for the Spirit of Harmony...
May all these things be found in you.

And that a Healing may begin within us each.

For a testimony of what Christ's Love can do.

Let these things be not without me...And most assuredly,
let these things be not without you!

LETTER I

Inspired 16 May 1990

The Necessity of the Return of God's Chosen People

May the Spirit of Truth speak—John 16:13

AND SO BEGINS A DIALOGUE—A perspective of unusual revelation concerning prophecy, ancient history's impact on current events, man's efforts for utopia, and his constant failures in the process. Man never gives up trying, from one social revolution to another, yet utopia seems to always be just one step away, waiting for this or that technological discovery to find it. Without recognizing God as his Creator, it is an endless and useless attempt by man to do without what he needs most. When things fall apart, man is smart enough to ask, "What went wrong?" But he is never patient enough to wait on God for the answer. We can see evidence of God through the constant beauty of nature, the witness of conscience, and the Bible.

It is no doubt that man is driven by a force—an opposing, unyielding, desperate, and angry force and a force which God has identified for us and to us. This deadly force realizes that God cannot get man to believe in Him as its ruler, so it causes man to doubt the True God through deceit. This is the art of deception, and enough men always take the bait.

My study of prophecy brings this deception to its fullest realization when I look into the history of the Jew, the ancient Hebrews, and the current Israelites, all God's chosen people. Without question, their history is the most glorious and yet painful of any people I know. I have witnessed these people, but only because they have been ordained by God to challenge this evil force, and though they have failed God in some respects, they have aided in saving mankind. The troubled birth of Isaac by Abraham and Sarah symbolizes this resistance to earthly affairs. God touched the seed of Isaac and commanded it to forever be a resistance, a sign post, and evidence of the true Creator and to reflect the limitations of the Law Principle and to save man.

The study of the Jew enduring constant persecution on a level unsurpassed and, in many cases, unfathomable will reveal even to the casual observer this force at its most potent form. God has used the Jew to show the world that there is an opposing force who is none other than Satan trying desperately to outdo God by exterminating the Jews.

The Jew is a people whose presence have always been treated with some disdain. In ancient history, they appear as the only centerpiece of the living God. Through their astounding belief in one God in antiquity, we see the gods of other nations, such as those created by the Romans, Greeks, Babylonians, etc., as man's imagination dictated by

Satan. These other gods were very real to the men of those days. They fought and died for them and even sacrificed their women and daughters in hopes of pleasing these imaginary beings. They never really existed. Unfortunately, they are to this day given more emphasis in schools and institutions of higher learning than the true living God is today. All children will learn about Zeus, under the guise of mythology, which in many cases has the audacity to include Jehovah.

It is extremely important to note that, after the resurrection of Jesus Christ, even the Romans who themselves aided in his crucifixion instituted Christianity in their kingdom as their religion. God had effectively shown man that He was, what He is, and that He shall forever be. The conclusion to all this is that this revelation to man about this most Supreme Being came at the expense of the Jew.

From Abraham to Jesus, a period of 1,700 years, God's masterful plan was to save man for a better day, if you will. Through prophecy, I saw that none of this was by accident. For Jesus Himself was prophesied by Moses almost a thousand years before his first coming. And so was the thirty pieces of silver he was sold for. And so was the potter's grave. And so was his clothes cast in the lot. And so was his persecutor, his own people, the Jew. None of this was a surprise whatsoever to God Himself. For by design, the Jew has shown us the kingdom of God, and that design is blueprinted by God, not orchestrated by the whimsicalness of man.

What would have happened if Jesus had lived to the ripe old age of one hundred, died of natural causes, been buried, and then resurrected? I shall tell you—He would have went unnoticed. As great as the resurrection of Lazarus was from the dead, such an act pales in comparison to the crucifixion of Jesus and his resurrection from a Roman-guarded grave blocked by a huge stone slab while the world watched. Satan's determination to prevent such a resurrection aided God's purpose in revealing to man a spiritual world beyond what we see, taste, smell, and hear.

Every bit of Jesus's life and death was prophesied. But where did the Jews as a people go wrong? Most of us are aware that Jesus was predicted in two forms—one as a suffering Messiah and the other as a reigning, glorious King. The Jews, "as a nation," could never figure out this double reference. Anyone in their human mind, Jew or Gentile, would want to be saved by a man of force, not a suffering Messiah. It would not be nearly as confusing if they took the prophets literally, accepted both, and not preferred one over the other. This is a classic case of the human viewpoint versus God's viewpoint. The Jews were only thinking of saving themselves for God's kingdom. On the other hand, God was planning to save all mankind, Jew and Gentile alike. Let's realize that "as a nation," any group of people would have made the same mistake after waiting almost a thousand years to be saved.

As prophesied, the city of Jerusalem and it's holy temple and Jewish citizens were officially destroyed and dispersed respectively in 70 AD. It was a worldwide dispersion and persecution, yet it had a worldwide survival rate. I thought Africans had it bad with colonization and economic slavery. I nearly cried for them after studying their history and recognizing their persecutor. But on May 14, 1948, the nation of Israel was restored, and it is prophesied that never shall they lose it. Journey with me through this phenomenal occurrence. These people had no land they could call their own from 70 AD to 1948, a total of 1,878 years. Think about what the world was then compared to now. The Jewish people were a minority everywhere they went. They had different languages, cultures, and environments to deal with. They never lost their "God-sent" identity, and they not only came back as a nation but got the very same most important strategically placed real estate called the Promised Land.

Once I marveled at this and accepted it as a literal biblical fact, I lost my identity as an African and saw myself as a Gentile, like days of old. For I knew God's chosen people were back, and based on prophecy, it is no accident. During my study on biblical prophecy, I found that God's will occurs just as it is written, but unfortunately, due to the valley of time, man's impatience rationalizes him to treat God's will symbolically. This can create a most serious error in interpreting God's Word.

To show just how literal God can be, listen to how He ordained the nation of Israel on November 2, 1917. On that date, the Balfour Declaration was issued. It certified British government support for the "establishment in Palestine of a national home for the Jewish people." This declaration was supported by the United States and was basically a settlement agreement. At that time, the area was occupied by the Turks and their German ally, who might resist such an act. British General Allenby was concerned—"Should they shell the city and risk damaging the holy sites?" He made it a matter of prayer and hit upon an unconventional idea. He had pilots drop leaflets on the city to urge peaceful surrender. The occupants evacuated the city on December 9, 1917, without one shot being fired. The Turks had occupied the area for over four hundred years and offered no resistance whatsoever.

Isaiah prophesied 2,500 years ago: "Like birds hovering overhead, the Lord Almighty will shield Jerusalem; he will shield it and deliver it, he will 'pass over' it and will rescue it" (Isaiah 31:5). So like hovering birds, the little biplanes were used by the Lord to defend Jerusalem. It was, in fact, protected, rescued, spared, and saved. Adding to the sense of mystery and evidence of God's hand guiding the events was the motto of the 14th Bomber Squadron whose planes were used to drop those leaflets: "I spread my wings and keep my promise."

On May 14, 1948, the nation of Israel was officially recognized throughout the world. The timing of this restoration when viewed objectively is most curious. During the early 1940s, mankind demonstrated to God two events which surpassed all of man's previous atrocities. One event was the anti-Semitism of a nation, handed out by Germany and known as the greatest Holocaust in all of history. The second event was the use of nuclear force by the United States on the Japanese cities of Nagasaki and Hiroshima. Both events were evidence that, given time, man could destroy himself.

One more bit of history concerns the city of Jerusalem. The city was a divided province up until the Arab-Israeli Six-Day War of 1967. The Jews were outnumbered and outgunned enormously, but miraculously the Jews captured the city and maintained military control over it. However, due to the great significance of Jerusalem as the Holy City for Islam, Christianity, and Judaism, the Jews did not have political control. Worldwide restraints orchestrated this limitation. But God prevailed nonetheless, and during the week of April 23, 1990, the Jews took full control and were able to announce Jerusalem as their state capital with sufficient United Nations support. And so "preparation" for the beginning of the Seventieth Week of Daniel was complete (Daniel 9:27).

In closing, the study of God's Prophetic Word reveals this—Man, blinded by his own self-righteousness, is failing to see God's righteousness, and the Christian church is no exception. The rebirth of Israel is not my word but God's. It's all over the Old Testament and noted in the "Valley of Dry Bones" in Ezekiel 37. In Romans 11, the "Olive Tree Parable," called a covenant by God, keeps their reality alive, and the Book of Revelations demands a Jewish gospel during the tribulation period (Revelation 7:1–8).

Be forewarned that, as the rise in anti-Semitism increases, the more evident God's presence shall be witnessed. At the signing of the covenant (our modern term: peace treaty), Daniel's Seventieth Week begins, and at that moment in God's plan, all will be Gentiles except for the Jew.

The final paradox is this: "Will the Gentiles make the same mistake against God's chosen people (Armageddon) as the Jews made against their own Messiah?"

God states, "Delusions shall be sent" (2 Thessalonians 2:10–12). I am beginning to understand His words as He so states them. If the Jew can be tested and persecuted so thoroughly for trying to please God through the Law and yet He uses their error to offer salvation to all Gentiles and even me, what right does the Gentile have to be left untried?

With this final revelation, I know I have found truth. I only seek to share this moment of spiritual enlightenment for the benefit of others. There is a voice in my mind which says, "Tell the people. Tell the people. Tell your people." Amen.

Gregory A. Booker

PS—So where is the Church of Christ during the Seventieth Week of Daniel (one week equals seven years)? Shall the Old Testament clash with the New Testament? Shall the 'Church of Christ' be subjected to the wrath of the Lord "in that day"? I offer you a word of comfort from 1 Thessalonians 4:15–18.

> "For this we say unto you by the word of the Lord, that we which are alive and remain unto the coming of the Lord shall not prevent them which are asleep. For the Lord Himself shall descend from heaven with a shout, with the voice of the archangel, and with the trump of God: and the dead in Christ shall rise first: Then we which are alive and remain shall be caught up together with them in the clouds, to meet the Lord in the air: and so shall we ever be with the Lord. Wherefore comfort one another with these words."

Thank you for your time. I only seek to plant a seed of concern, with all due respect to your ministry. All these things I mentioned are a prerequisite to the second coming of Jesus Christ, our Lord and Savior, and the final blessing for the remnant of Israel throughout the ages.

LETTER II

Inspired 22 November 1990

Prophecy is Alive and Well, and Israel is the Key

THE FOLLOWING HIGHLIGHTS ARE FROM Romans 11, also known as "The Olive Tree Parable."

- Is Israel cast away forever? God forbid.
- God foreknew Israel's error.
- Christianity is "contrary to nature."
- Christians are warned to not be conceited and boastful.
- God reveals "until the fullness of the Gentiles comes in," implying a period of termination.
- And so Israel shall be saved.

Israel is the root. Christianity is the branches. (Note: Many other religions have also grown as branches from the root by condemning the Jews for their error. Most notable is Islam.) For Israel, hope is eternal. And their final blessings be the greater for all mankind.

Conclusion: Mankind, be forewarned.

God's grace upon the Gentiles exists only as long as Israel does not. Israel was restored as a nation on May 14, 1948. Those two facts are indeed mutually exclusive. God will not favor both Jew and Gentile at the same time due to spiritual contradiction as reflected by prophecy. First and Second Thessalonians details an event known as the rapture. First Corinthians 15:51–58 further supports such an occurrence. The significance of a "sudden disappearance of believers in Christ" is to officially close Christ's ministry on Earth so that God may continue with the fulfillment of the redemption of Israel through repentance and ultimately Israel calling for their Messiah out of desperation. This calling is a technical requirement Israel has yet to fulfill in order to bring the literal return of Christ.

With the restoration of Israel, the potential for God's Word to fulfill itself unbeknownst to the world, including self-righteous religious leaders, is becoming all too clear. It was also prophesied that Israel would once again take possession of Jerusalem. Under much world opposition, the Jews were able to reclaim control and call it their capital in April 1990. Even to the most novice observer, Israel's return as a nation after approximately two thousand years of non-existence is simply miraculous. I, however, give credit to God and God alone, since He revealed such in the Bible over 2,500 years ago and restates it profoundly throughout the New Testament. Let's also consider the fact that it's the very same, most important, strategically placed piece of real estate called the Promised Land. Coincidence?

Let me say this—the Holy Spirit has indeed spoken to me revealing what is to come. But it is only because I made it clear in my prayers to God that I wanted truth no matter how difficult it may be to believed. And such truth was given to me. I studied long and hard to objectively understand the necessity of the return of God's chosen people. I now know that from God's perspective, dare I say, that the long-awaited promises made to the many servants of God from the nation of Israel are rightfully due. Consider the root of the Olive Tree Parable. And consider this—All men stand to be in error against Israel and ultimately against God Himself if they know not the truth.

The final paradox mentioned in my first letter was "Will the Gentiles make the same mistake against God's chosen people (Armageddon) as the Jews made against their own Messiah?" The answer is a resounding "Yes!" This paradox explains why the Book of Revelations is written and why the battle of Armageddon will indeed be fulfilled in the Valley of Jehoshaphat, just outside of the most Holy City on Earth—Jerusalem.

Be forewarned that God states, "Delusions shall be sent" (2 Thessalonians 2:9–11). This warning means that without the knowledge of truth, our liberalistic attitudes about God become self-righteous and suspect if the literal Word of God is forsaken. As the "delusions" challenge man's belief in the things of God, an interesting phenomenon occurs. The different "liberal beliefs" of man are beginning to form a universal thought which conflicts with truth itself. God's delusions are the tools which actually begin the process of separating the wheat from the tares. Be forewarned.

So that you may know the truth of the Lord, I appeal to you to review certain prophetic biblical sections of the Bible for your own enrichment concerning what the world is going through in these most trying times. The following are the most profound:

MATTHEW 24 (Spoken approx. 30 AD)

Jesus foretells the signs of His coming and how it coincides with the end of the world. The key verse is verse 15 which refers to the Book of Daniel.

DANIEL 9:22–27 (Written 535 BC)

Matthews 24:15 cites verse 27 of Daniel 9. This unfulfilled week (one week equals seven years) is known as the Seventieth Week of Daniel. All scholars recognize this week as literally unique unto Israel. Notice that a covenant will be made with someone else for the seven-year period. I ask you this: "What is the world insisting on Israel to do?" Is it not to agree to settle for peace? The modern synonym of "covenant" is indeed peace treaty. Potential!!! The key verse is verse 27.

REVELATIONS 11:2 AND 13:5 (Written approx. 96 AD)

Revelations is the only book in the Bible which measures itself by time. Notice the mention of forty-two months and another forty-two months of rule by "him to continue." Eighty-four months divided by twelve equals seven years. This concludes that, when Israel and someone else sign a peace settlement, man has seven years of this world as we know it before the second coming of Christ. Revelations is also the time Matthew 24 and Daniel's Seventieth Week is referring to.

EZEKIEL 34, 36, AND 37 (Written approx. 580 BC)

These chapters are the clearest, most definitive evidence of the restoration of modern Israel, commonly known as the "Valley of Dry Bones."

EZEKIEL 35, 38, AND 39 (Written approx. 580 BC)

These chapters cover the type and character of the people and nations who will surround Israel at their rebirth. Mount Seir (Edomites) is the location of the Arab countries. Notice the words "perpetual hatred." How true those words are today. Also, the Land of Gog is the Soviet Union (a.k.a. "land of the uttermost north") and their republics. Even quite a few African nations have been backed by anti-Semitic rhetoric. The most obvious is that they all are highly anti-Semitic. These biblical battles are unfulfilled to date, but do they not have tremendous potential to be realized?

2 TIMOTHY 3 AND 4; 2 PETER 3:1–8; 2 PETER 2:1–2, 2 THESSALONIANS 2:3, 9–12; AND ROMANS 1

The immoral and deviant character of man in the last days is illustrated in these passages. God knows His creation and the signs of an Apostate Church of unbelief in God as He has been known.

Man today is too "modern" to consider ancient words as having any meaning for current events. Remember this, Jesus Christ is the only Messiah who God approved for man in order to someday be in God's eternal kingdom. Man is growing weary of faith and faith alone in God since man has spent two thousand years waiting. There are many more biblical verses that reiterate all that has been told to you. Be forewarned that anti-Semitism which is on the rise throughout the world is the tool of God's adversary, Satan.

I have often asked the question, "Why has the nation of Israel received no glory for their blood, sweat, and tears as inspired by their relationship with God, yet by their error, were we, "the Gentiles," saved without being put to the test as they were?" This is what the Holy Spirit has allowed me to see, but only because I asked the question.

I now know that God's righteousness is pure and just. There is indeed a spiritual battle in the midst. Who would resist Christ's second coming more than anyone else? None more than Satan who can work his deception on anyone who is unaware of the truth from God Himself. I glorify in the magnificence of such a God who is master of our souls and offers eternal life to all who overcome and accept His only begotten Son as our Lord and Savior Jesus Christ, the Messiah. Let his atonement for our sins be not in vain.

In closing, the study of God's Prophetic Word reveals this—Man, blinded by his own self-righteousness, is failing to see God's righteousness. There is a voice in my mind which says, "Tell the people. Tell the people. Tell your people." Amen! (John 16:13 and 2 Peter 1:18–21)

Gregory A. Booker

PS—IF YOU FEAR THE QUESTION, you stand never to receive the answer, and the answer is only as good as the question you ask. I have given you an answer, although you have asked me no question. I only seek to plant a seed of concern. Thank you.

Spiritual insight: Israel's hope is in the Olive Tree Parable. May this be wisdom—

- It is most clear that the State of Israel and their possession of the Holy City of Jerusalem is a biblical requirement precluding the Book of Revelations.
- It is most clear that the signing of a covenant with Israel will identify the Antichrist (leader of a Ten-Nation Confederacy) and the False Prophet (leader of Israel). In addition, it represents the final seven years of this current age known as the Church Age. The Book of Revelations is officially opened at the sign-

ing of the covenant. At the end of the seven-year period, the Day of Redemption shall be realized for Israel, ushering in the millennial kingdom for all other believers in the one True God and His Son, Jesus Christ. Thus, it is written in 1 Thessalonians 5:1–6, "But of the times and the seasons, brethren, ye have no need that I write unto you. For yourselves know perfectly that the day of the Lord so cometh as a thief in the night. For when they shall say, Peace and safety; then sudden destruction cometh upon them…and they shall not escape. But ye, brethren, are not in darkness, that that day should overtake you as a thief. Ye are all children of the light…nor of darkness. Therefore, let us not sleep, as do others; but let us watch and be sober." And this is the kingdom to come. "And God shall wipe away all tears from their eyes; and there shall be no more death, neither sorrow, nor crying, neither shall there be any more pain: for the former things are passed away. And he that sat upon the throne said, Behold, I make all things new" (Revelation 21:4–5).

- Caution: For the Gentile error shall be "Thou works shall support faith, but faith in what? For can it not be obscured without truth as it's mentor and grace as its final gift." Remember, did not the Jews have all the faith in the world concerning the first coming of Jesus and yet persecute him? For by the Law they sought to achieve grace and failed. So is not the Gentile full of faith and, if not careful, using his works to justify receipt of God's grace? The final word is grace is given, not earned, and given by permission, not owed through works.

- Just like Jesus's first coming—poor and dressed in sackcloth—the Jews were so deluded, except for a remnant. So shall the Gentiles be deluded by the "False Persona" of the nation of Israel. They shall take it upon themselves to destroy God's chosen people, except for a remnant—the raptured (Church of Christ) and the tested (Tribulation Saints). And so Israel will repent out of desperation with nowhere to turn but to Jesus, and Israel shall be saved and so shall man. *As the Jew, so is the Gentile!*

INSPIRED WRITINGS

AND THEY WALK WITH THEIR HEADS DOWN
A Vision of the Cross

SO THERE WE GO, ALL of us walking through life, feet slow with our step being guided, but not knowing where. Heads down. All heads are down. Millions upon millions, walking a slow but steady pace. For some unknown reason, many are afraid to look up, but they do look at something if only to walk around it, lest they bump into the obstacle.

The walk of mankind is the fear in Adam. "I heard the voice of the Lord in the garden, and I was afraid because I was naked, and so I hid myself." And the Lord said, "Who told thee thou was naked?"

Adam never did answer the question of who told him he was naked. He seemed too anxious to place blame when what was needed was admitting fault! Yes, this is the walk of mankind. In the garden, the obstacle was the voice of the Lord, but on Calvary's hill, the obstacle is none other than the cross. And all mankind travels the path of life with this obstacle in their way. This is my vision at the cross.

Mankind travels the path that leads ultimately to Calvary's hill. God has predestined man to walk this path, but man decides whether he shall travel it, looking up, looking at the cross, or not even looking at all. I walked such a walk, but now a vision is given unto me. The cross is at the top of the hill, unmovable by time, and none can remove it, though they may try. So heads are down and souls are hid as they walk the path that is laid down before them. Each man senses that something is in the path of his way. Most will simply follow the path that others beside them walk. Seeking not to question, they receive no answers.

As they approach the cross, most walk around it without even looking up, let alone looking at. As they merge back together after being split by the presence of the cross in the middle of the hill, they do look back to see what caused them to split. And when they do look up at the back of the cross, they see no one! Thinking themselves the wiser, they walk in their pride, unashamed of their sins. Since they see no Christ on the cross, they see no need for salvation. It is the time they choose to look up that blinds them. This is religion!

And then there are those who look at the cross, failing to look up at the Christ. They see the stake in the road and lean against it to rest. They find that the stake is comforting, and they raise their hands, assimilating the posture of the One above them. Hence, they become a fair distraction as multitudes upon multitudes pass by. They do attract a great many who stop to soothe their bowed heads that they might not hide with closed eyes. They admit that Someone is nailed to the cross. "Better Him than me," they say. Being at the base of the cross, they have no need to pick up their cross and deny themselves for they are too busy attracting others to its base. No need to climb up when we can just stay down. The Spirit acknowledges these as the institution of Christianity. They have the knowledge of the Word, but they do not give their heart to Christ.

And then there are those who, as they walk in the crowd, as they stand at the base of the cross, for some unknown reason, look up, gazing in amazement at the bloodied disfigured man nailed to the cross. They search the cross for all its purpose, but more significantly, they react to its error, for He was found without Sin in His body and undeserving of the death man placed upon Him. Thus we are found guilty of what we already were... sinners! These, they hide no more from the voice the cross represents. They fall to their knees, recognizing that they should be nailed to the cross, and therein is found the grace of God and so they repent!

The Spirit of the cross then lifts me up and sets me out of the multitudes and on the sideline. Eyes are open and my head is straight, and I am told to beckon to the crowd to "Look up... Look up!" But only so few do as they walk with heads down. To carry your cross, you must be willing to be placed upon it! This is the victory, and this is the vision I was made to see, and these on the sidelines are the sealed!

LETTER III

Inspired first week of April 1991

The Paradox of the Seventieth Week of Daniel

AFTER THE ANGEL OF THE Lord revealed to Daniel, the prophet, the future of mankind and Israel in particular, Daniel reflects on his dismay at not understanding God's revelations. In Daniel 12, the angel directs Daniel to "Shut up the words, and seal the book" and "Go thy way, Daniel: for the words are closed up and sealed till the time of the end."

After the apostle Paul reveals, through the Holy Spirit, divine knowledge concerning the relationship between Jew and Gentile in the Olive Tree Parable of Romans 11, Paul praises God's plan. In verse 33, he writes, "O the depth of the riches both of the wisdom and knowledge of God! How unsearchable are his judgments, and his ways past finding out!"

The Book of Revelations reveals the angelic realm applauding the Lord and the Lamb (Jesus) for their long-suffering patience and love toward all men...but now the time has come. And John, the writer of the book, is a witness of who is worthy to judge mankind. (See Revelations 4 and 5.)

So when the time has come, who will be worthy to judge and what is the criteria for such worthiness? The Book of Revelations gives the honor and the glory of such worthiness to Jesus Christ. Why? The answer is simple—he earned it! Can we say that there has only been one individual who was crucified unjustly and without mercy yet did not commit one sin? The True God states the penalty for sin is death. Jesus, therefore, did not deserve to die. This is the very reason Jesus was resurrected and the very reason why He and He alone is worthy to judge and defeat his real adversary, Satan, and unfortunately, man in his unbelief. This is the centerpiece of truth.

Let us now know the verdict of the Lord. It is best that I open this revelation about the future by reflecting on the past. For it is understood that if one is to determine the accuracy of prophecy, modern man can do so perhaps better than any other generation. I have discovered the prophetic Word of God to be without error. While predicting when events occur is the popular definition, it is by no means the most significant. The greater purpose of prophecy is to interpret the results of key events in accordance with divine will, by far the more difficult task to perform.

There are two historical facts which must be brought to the forefront that I recognize as paramount to understanding truth. Before I address the main topic, I recommend all to consider what should be obvious, but is not, concerning the following two key observations.

THE JEWISH BURDEN

"I will gather them that are sorrowful for the solemn assembly, who are of thee, to whom the reproach of it was a burden" (Zephaniah 3:18).

"I [Israel] will bear the indignation of the Lord, because I have sinned against him, until he plead my cause, and execute judgment for me: he will bring me forth to the light, and I shall behold his righteousness" (Micah 7:9).

"And it shall come to pass, that as ye were a curse among the heathen..." (Zechariah 8:13).

And, it is written in the New Testament in Romans 11:11— "I say then, Have they stumbled that they should fall? God forbid: but rather through their fall salvation is come unto the Gentiles, for to [eventually] provoke them [Israel] to jealousy."

I ASK ALL—WHO ARE THE writers of the Bible? Are they not the Jews?

I ask all—Whose experiences do the Christian churches depend on? Is it not the biblical characters and are they also Jewish?

I ask all—Whose errors have been used for our benefit? Is it not Israel's?

And one final observation—Who had the responsibility of measuring up to God's standards and documenting the results without bias for all the world to see while the Gentiles continued in their sins? None other than the Jews by the election of God Himself!

It should become clear what is being stressed. Every Sunday, Christian churches depend upon the Jewish relationship to God in understanding how all men must relate to Him. It is a blessed honor to the Jewish people, but God knew it would also create a special curse upon them. And so it has, as history reveals (notice how truth demonstrates itself prophetically).

Through the ordainment of God, the Jews have given the Gentiles the Bible. What have the Gentiles given in return? That is the question with no real answer. Therefore, no one on this planet should be prejudice against the Jew. However, even in the Christian churches, anti-Semitism is indeed present. Case in point—As different as the Roman Catholic Church is from Islam, guess what they both agree on? Neither recognize Jewish Zionism rights! And though they have different reasons, it is the same conclusion that is alarming.

I now understand why God told us about Israel in the Abrahamic Covenant in Genesis 12:3—"I will bless them that bless thee, and curse him that curseth thee." The verse continues with "and in thee shall all families of the earth be blessed."

The gospel of Christ has reached across the globe to include men and women around the world, a proof of the prophetic Word of God proving His reality. History supports this phenomenon. Their contributions have aided God in revealing to man all we know of the True God, unaware of it themselves. Let us as Christians recognize and accept God's chosen people who have been burdened by the necessary work of the Lord. Their burden has been our gain. This fact actually proves beyond a shadow of a doubt that there is a very real and very awesome eternal Supreme Being among us…Amen!

We must understand Israel's rebirth in May 1948 and the continuing exodus of the Jews from around the world as a preparation for their final blessing. We must also understand why they have been so often falsely accused. I won't hesitate to say that this deception could have satanic origin, and so I forewarn all. Here is where the Spirit of Truth reveals a very dark secret. Satan, through the weakness of men, has continuously sought to invalidate the prophetic Word of God by attempting to destroy the Jews. If a man has no love for his neighbor, he has no love for truth. And no matter what faith he has, he stands to be in error when truth is demonstrated by God Himself. The Jewish burden is very real; therefore, I know their blessing will be also. First the Jew and then the Gentiles!

Envy has no place here.

PARADOX DEFINED

IT IS VERY IMPORTANT THAT the meaning of "paradox" is understood. Webster defines it as "A proposition contrary to received opinion; also an assertion seemingly contradictory or opposed to common sense but may yet be true in fact."

The word "paradox" has the perfect application to Christ's first coming when the Jews refused to believe He was their Messiah sent by God. Shall the Gentiles make the same mistake, failing to recognize Christ's second coming and relying on their own wisdom? And would it be fair to test the Jew and not also the Gentile? It is written that God foreknew the error of the Jews. He, therefore, I assure you, foreknows the error of the Gentiles. Be forewarned.

Oh, the magnificence of the Lord! He has indeed blessed me to "see" His Word so clearly. I sought out the truth, and he has given it abundantly. May you also be blessed by the reading of these words.

THE WEEK

LET US NOW BEGIN A study on "The Week," also known as the tribulation period.

- In the latter times
- The day of the Lord (to mankind)
- The time of Jacob's trouble (to Israel)
- The Book of Revelation (to the Church)

Without being too technical, I will highlight what the Seventieth Week of Daniel is. Chapter 9 of the Book of Daniel, dated approximately 530 BC, reflects Daniel praying, desiring to know what God's future dealings with Israel are. Gabriel, the messenger, comes to answer his prayer, giving him skill and understanding. Verse 24 states, "Seventy weeks are determined upon thy people and upon thy holy city [Jerusalem]." These weeks are based on the Jewish sabbatical week of years described in Leviticus 25 where each week equals seven years times seventy weeks which equals 490 years. Daniel 9:24 continues by revealing the fulfillment of conditions at the conclusion of the 490-year period of God's jurisdiction. These conditions as stated are:

1. To finish the transgression.
2. To make an end of sins.
3. To make reconciliation for iniquity.
4. To bring in everlasting righteousness.
5. To seal up the vision and prophecy.
6. And to anoint the most Holy.

Verses 25 and 26 reveal what will happen from the "commandment to restore …Jerusalem" to when "shall Messiah be cut off." This time span covered exactly sixty-nine weeks or 483 years (based on the Jewish calendar of 360 days per year). The balance of verse 26 details the destruction of the sanctuary (Jewish Temple) which occurred in 70 AD. This represented God's abandonment of his people for their error committed against their Messiah.

Verses 25 and 26 were fulfilled as written. I researched the events in great detail to confirm such. At times, God's revelations can be so complex, but even for the less studious person, He makes His plan simple. If you don't understand one thing I've revealed, go back to the conditions stated in verse 24 and ask yourself, "Have any of these conditions been yet fulfilled?" Even the most simpleminded would say, "No! Of course not, because there is 'one week' unaccounted for." History reveals the Jewish dispersion from 70 AD to 1948 with no restoration between.

Verse 27 has one week outstanding which is to be confirmed by a covenant. At this point, we know one week equals seven years and that an agreement will be made with Israel and someone else known as "he." I consider verse 27 to be a technical verse because it implies so much, but I will strive to maintain simplicity.

Now notice, verse 27 continues "…in the midst of the week he shall cause the sacrifice…to cease." What sacrifice? This reference implies far more than the average person realizes. It demands the Jews exist as a nation (they possess Jerusalem) so that they may rebuild their Temple. Then they can perform their sacrifices once again before the Lord. However, "he" who signed the agreement (probably a treaty of protection) with Israel will break his agreement in the midst (at three-and-a-half years). He will stop Jewish worship to the Lord and will proclaim Himself to be God. He will stand in the holy place (the Holy of Holies, situated only in the Jewish Temple). This is the abomination of desolation spoken of and the "he" who performs the act is the Antichrist.

Let me again state that what I truly seek to reveal is the potential for key events to occur. Currently, there are strong undercurrents to begin a serious attempt at discussing and achieving peace with Israel and the Arabs. I am convinced that this "week" has yet to begin but is probable within a few years or even sooner.

The next key element is the issue of the Jews determination to rebuild their temple. Again, I stress it is the interpretation of events that is critical. For example, on October 9, 1990, twenty Palestinians were killed. A news article reported that there "was a rumor that a small group of Jewish radicals were planning to lay a cornerstone for a new Jewish temple on the sanctuary where the Moslem Mosque stands." The issue of whether the Israelis used excessive force, as in defending themselves, may never be known. However, Israel's last and only ally, the United States, was caught in a political bind and weakened because of the Arab coalition participants in Desert Storm. The US agreed with the majority, condemning Israel for its "act of aggression," overlooking Israel's claims. I am sure the US position with Israel was further fractured by the selling of weapons to the Arab coalition members in opposing Iraq. I assure you that the Arabs are ironically in a greater position collectively to challenge Israel than before Desert Storm. This is just one of the examples of how complex and contrary things really are.

To demonstrate further in Ezekiel 35:1–5, Ezekiel is told to prophecy against Mount Seir. Earlier Scripture identifies such as the land of the Edomites, the ancient tribal name for the modern Arabs. Verses 5 and 7 read, "Because thou has had a perpetual hatred, and hast shed the blood of the children of Israel by the force of the sword in the time of their calamity...Thus will I make Mount Seir most desolate." This chapter is in the midst of prophetic information revealing Israel's rebirth (Ezekiel 34, 36, and 37).

Official reports state that of the approximately twenty Arab nations, thirteen of them have a policy of annihilation against Israel. But through the prophet Zechariah, it is written, "Behold, the day of the Lord cometh...For I will gather all nations against Jerusalem to battle; and the city shall be taken, and the houses rifled, and the women ravished; and half of the city shall go forth into captivity, and the residue of the people shall not be cut off from the city. Then shall the Lord go forth, and fight against those nations, as when he fought in the day of battle. And his feet shall stand in that day upon the mount of Olives, which is before Jerusalem" (Zechariah 14:1–4).

I do not mean to imply that Israel is not without its own faults. The Lord does not favor unbelief in either Jew or Gentile (See Zechariah 13:8–9.). For the vengeance truly is the Lord's for He shall repay (Romans 12:19). The "children of disobedience" have been blinded by the ruler of this world, and Satan is as an Angel of Light and is the father of all lies. Yes, it is sad that such hate exists against a nation such as Israel, considering all its contributions to man's salvation. I am convinced that it can only be deception at its finest orchestrated by the adversary to God...for a time, just a little more time, and "he" knows it.

Jesus references "The Week" in Matthew 24:15. Almost six hundred years after the prophets, He speaks a direct statement to its further fulfillment still pending. No act of desecration of any kind in the temple occurred during the destruction of the temple in 70 AD by the Romans. Neither did the world end, nor did Christ return, which is the question Jesus is answering in Matthew 24.

In fact, if one looks closely at Matthew 24:22, you will realize that Christ is not coming to destroy the world but to save it—"Except those days should be shortened, there should no flesh be saved: but for the elect's sake those days shall be shortened." He will, however, defeat those who resist His coming. It is strange that such a glorious opportunity for man will be lost to many. I forewarn all while yet there is time. For Jesus states..."Behold, I have told you before!" (Matthew 24:25).

Shall we now know the future?

The word "repentance" is defined as "to change one's mind or one's heart with regard to past or intended action or conduct on account of regret; a genuine request for forgiveness as a result of great sorrow; based on an acknowledgment of fault or error and desiring forgiveness of the transgression."

ISRAEL'S CURRENT SPIRITUAL CONDITION

IT IS WRITTEN, THAT WHEN Israel is restored, that they "as a nation" will still be in unbelief concerning Jesus. Their blindness continues as prophesied. And so it is...in fact, the Jews who do believe in Christ (a tiny minority) are excluded from automatic citizenship in their own homeland of Israel! News articles reveal the majority of Jews that are in Israel call themselves Humanistic Jews: "A growing international movement where the desire is to have a temple with a congregation and a rabbi where no one believes in God." Without question, they are lost. A required redemption proves their blindness.

Another class of Jews that have residence in Israel, though in the minority, are the Orthodox Jews. It is the Orthodox Jew who reads at least the Old Testament books, performs the Mosaic Laws, and continues to wait on their Messiah, yet rejects Jesus. Therefore, could it be reasoned that it is they who will ultimately repent when placed under the duress of the Antichrist? For as Jesus forewarned, or can we say prophesied, the Jews would reject Him.

Jesus speaking prophetically states in Matthew 23:38–39…"Behold, your house is left unto you desolate. For I say unto you, Ye shall not see me henceforth, till ye shall say, Blessed is he that cometh in the name of the Lord." Could Israel's rejection require Israel's repentance? Is this what our Lord and Savior, Jesus Christ, waits for? His grace abounds! Oh…but *the Jew's unbelief in God is not just among themselves!*

THE MYSTERY OF THE GENTILES

AND HERE IS WISDOM—GENTILES CAN easily identify the Jew, but few people, whether White, Black, Indian, Arab, Chinese, Russian, American, Cuban, or anything else "see" themselves as all in one group— Gentiles!!! Dare I say that this is the only way God sees us? He always has and always will. This is the barrier I crossed, and I heard the angels applaud my vision of spiritual clarity. For it is the Gentiles with each having their own pride that blinds themselves. "Little Pharisees" would be the perfect representation from God's viewpoint.

There is so much divisiveness among the Gentiles, including Christians, that one will not hear the other, even if it is the truth. The question "What is truth?" has been answered and proven. It is unbelief that blinds. For it is written in 2 Thessalonians 2:3, "Let no man deceive you by any means: for that day [Day of Christ] shall not come, except there come a falling away first, and that man of sin be revealed, the son of perdition." Due to the religious pluralism among the Gentiles, the field is ripe for an erosion of biblical principles and a conclusive "falling away" by Christianity to also take on an apostate form of unbelief!

AND MAY THIS BE WISDOM

THE UNBELIEF OF GENTILES WILL open the eyes of Israel to call for their Messiah, who they first rejected, and Israel shall be saved. While most men believe in a god, the True God asks all to believe in His work, a very real work—Jesus. What good is faith in God if you ignore His Perfect Work? And that's the catch! Do you see the paradox?

THE RIGHTEOUSNESS OF THE LORD DEMONSTRATED

THE WORD "APOSTASY" IS DEFINED as "an abandonment of what one has voluntarily professed; a total desertion or departure from one's faith, principles, and beliefs; also, one who has forsaken his religion for another."

A one-world religion to come is no secret to a lot of Christians, but what form will it take? I have but a glimpse of what I see forming on the horizon. May it give you vision and strengthen your walk with Jesus above all.

I will briefly discuss two events—one which is obvious and the other which is not so obvious. First is the issue of permitting gay priests to preach. In the early 1990s, the Roman Catholic Church gave in to the mounting pressures of humanistic choice. A statement from the leaders allowed gay ministry if the congregation voted their approval. Even in the Protestant branch, the issue is being considered. Recent news broadcasts reveal the Episcopalians and Presbyterian denominations will discuss their rationale this summer. It should not even be an issue, but it is.

The second event is but a whisper now but do I see far more. There is a group of religious leaders—experts, mind you—who are selling the idea that "as long as Jerusalem and Palestine are viewed as Holy Land and Promised Land, rather than secular and geographic territory, we will never have a peaceful settlement in the Middle East. We have to de-sacralize and de-biblicize Jerusalem and Palestine." I ask all who called it the Promised Land? Did not the Lord Himself? Is man employing sound doctrine? And just what is de-biblicize? Could it mean to "take out" biblical references, denying God's truths openly and conclusively? These "religious leaders" covered a variety of Christian denominations. Their opinions can cause so many others to follow. Be forewarned. The real problem is if you are not sure of truth, how can you be sure of what is not truth?

For it is written "Even as there shall be false teachers among you, who shall bring in damnable heresies, even denying the Lord that brought them" (2 Peter 2:1).

"While they promise them liberty, they themselves are the servants of corruption...For if after they have escaped the pollutions of the world through the knowledge of the Lord and Savior Jesus Christ, they are again entangled therein, and overcome, the latter end is worse with them than the beginning. For it had been better for them not to have known the way of righteousness, than, after they had known it, to turn from the holy commandment delivered unto them" (2 Peter 2:19–21).

CONCLUSION

Spiritual insight concerning the "signing of the covenant" acts as a covenant of condemnation upon man. Giving two classes of unbelievers what they want by permitting their religious apostasy to be expressed and formalized conclusively in Israel's ultimate peace treaty, both the Jew and the Gentile are dealt with collectively. The Lord plays no favorites, but He will use one to achieve the other.

Case in point—God states in Zechariah 13:8–9 that one-third of the Jews shall be saved, meaning two-thirds will be lost. This means that it will take the loss of two-thirds of the Jews before they recognize their blindness and repent, turning to Jesus to be saved and not by their own effort or weapons. God will allow Satan to gather all unbelieving Gentiles to attempt to destroy all the Jews. Anti-Semitism will escalate dramatically as time moves on. The Messiah shall indeed come down at His calling and redeem Israel. And does this not indeed "provoke Israel to jealousy" (Romans 11:11)? This process actually aids God in passing judgment on man and his unbelief in the literal Word of the Lord.

Do you see the paradox? Oh, much has been said, perhaps the unexpected, perhaps the unwanted, perhaps the nerve, but most of all, perhaps the truth. The art of deception is to be blind to being deceived. History reveals that unbelievers make the prophetic Word of God become so true.

Do you see why such a noble cause as a "peace treaty" is determined to represent the opening of the Book of Revelations? Do you see the paradox of the Seventieth Week of Daniel?

Let it be said that the Lord always gives us hope. Let us receive of it!

For it is written in 1 Corinthians 14:3, "But he that prophesieth speaketh unto men to edification, and exhortation, and comfort." I have edified the church. May I now conclude with exhortation and comfort.

EXHORTATION

ONE OF THE MAIN VIEWPOINTS of the true Christian is to recognize God's election of His chosen people to reach out to the world to save mankind so that all can partake of His promise to restore man to his original condition before the fall of Adam. This is God's ultimate goal, and He sets the conditions. Unfortunately, there is an adversary to God, and Adam, in utilizing his free will, became subject to him. Christ defeated the adversary by dying sinless on the cross.

God states all men are sinners and that's the only reason we die. His code of righteousness shall not waver, and his love for us is even greater as demonstrated by Christ. Due to the virgin birth, Christ was not born a sinner but had the challenge of becoming a sinner since he was of the flesh. He committed no sin, so the question should be why was he so viciously crucified? The answer—Satan himself was trying, through the weakness of men, to make Christ commit just one sin. Be it cursing, showing pride, or finally striking back. Jesus succeeded by doing none of these.

Jesus certified the righteousness and the love of God, justifying men through their faith in Christ and making us qualified to enter into that eternal kingdom at the appointed time. Yes, the eternal life lost in Adam is now regained by the sacrifice of Christ on the cross. Thus, it is written in 1 Corinthians 2:7–8, "But we speak the wisdom of God in a mystery, even the hidden wisdom, which God ordained before the world unto our glory: Which none of the princes of this world knew: for had they known it, they would not have crucified the Lord of glory." Oh, the wisdom of the Lord exposed the pride of the adversary and "Therefore thou art inexcusable, O man, whosoever thou art that judgest" (Romans 2:1).

Now God is restoring Israel to receive the promises made to the many servants of the Lord from that nation. When Israel calls their Messiah, they will be saved. I forewarn all that the darkest hour is about to come on man. This generation can look backward and measure the words of God, but too few do. I have done so, and I see a mighty God soon to reveal Himself. Think of ancient words fulfilling themselves and there is nothing we can do about it. This kind of power is immeasurable by the human mind. I am not afraid to admit that we, myself included, are but pawns given an opportunity to someday stand before

Him per His terms. God knows we cannot be perfect (though we keep trying). That's why he gave us an example of perfection and asked us to believe in His Perfect Work as He demonstrated it.

There is plenty of "self-righteousness doctrine" pretending to be right, even in the Christian church. If I may state my opinion on the matter, the problem with Christianity is it's "personality." It ain't Christ—and I mean just that...ain't! We should seek to live like and in Christ, but do we? I'm not passing judgment, but time is of the essence. Therefore, let us pray for a strong back, just in case we are given a heavy load to bare.

I SEEK TO COMFORT BY MY PERSONAL TESTIMONY

JESUS REVEALS, "THE FATHER...SHALL GIVE you another Comforter... Even the Spirit of Truth; whom the world cannot receive, because it seeth him not...I will not leave you comfortless: I will come to you... But the Comforter, which is the Holy Ghost...sent in my name, he shall teach you all things, and bring all things to your remembrance" (John 14:16–18, 26). And so He surely has!

And finally, as a personal testimony, I desire to let it be known that, at this point in time, I am called to speak in the office of a prophet. I found this calling hard to believe at first and have come to accept it, realizing that it is a burden, but oh...is it a burden of joy! I sought truth out as Proverbs 2:1–9 instructed, and I know that wisdom and knowledge are more precious than gold as Proverbs 3:13–20 reveals. So for no price or purchase do I give to others what has been freely given to me.

This man has learned to cry again for mankind, regardless of the color of one's skin, his political beliefs, his criminal record, his irreligious principals, and his customs, and regardless of his hate for truth. Man is lost, but he is who Jesus died for, so who am I to judge. I know not the day, but I glorify in the coming Messiah to redeem Israel...and man. And so should all, for at that time, Jew and Gentile who do believeth shall eat at the same table and serve the same Lord.

I have prayed to God to feed me so that I may feed others. He has graciously answered my prayers. However, I do feel the Holy Spirit has given me such intimate answers only because the time is so near. For when the Hand of God can be revealed from beginning to it's very end and still mankind does not heed...What then? Thus, it is written in

1 Corinthians 2:12–13, "Now we have received, not the spirit of the world, but the spirit which is of God; that we might know the things that are freely given to us of God. Which things also we speak, not in the words which man's wisdom teacheth, but which the Holy Spirit teacheth; comparing spiritual things with spiritual." This is the wisdom and the hope that I proclaim to all that have an ear!

Therefore, when you have a measure of faith and just a little understanding, pray for a sign to confirm what I write. I am not above being tested, and I have sought confirmation myself and have received a confirming sign of supernatural origin. If your heart is open and you are overcome with joy concerning the secrets I reveal, then all I ask is this—what I have given to you, do the same. Give a copy to another. Share. I know that's what God really asks of us, for it is the best way to demonstrate faith and above all, love.

Yes. the true Rainbow Coalition are those who follow Christ, thereby overcoming their biases. If you fully follow the commandment of "Love thy neighbor as thyself," you won't find yourself being prejudice and ultimately opposed to what God is doing. Yes, the prophetic Word of God states that in the last days "Love shall wax cold!" I forewarn that you may also be forearmed and not surprised, lest you are caught unaware and unprepared. Therefore, stand and be unmovable in your faith. And may your faith be found in Christ and Christ only!

I thank God for His patience, for He has indeed been long-suffering toward us, But there comes a time, and perhaps the time has come. Indeed, can we say the time is in this generation? If so be it, I stand, even in my trials, I stand on the shoulders of the prophets and shout their words. Amen and Amen!!!

Gregory A. Booker

INSPIRED WRITINGS

GREETINGS, MINISTERS OF THE CHURCHES AND THE CONGREGATION

THE WORD IS DECLARED, AND the moment has been established. This is the "times of restitution" bringing forth the coming of our Lord and Savior, the Christ. If the apostles can declare it, then why, with all we are made to see, cannot we declare it now? By the grace of God, there is one who works in the "office of a prophet" in the house of the Lord. The Lord has found him, one who is determined to speak the prophetic Word of God, for I am commanded to publish these words before the congregation that they might know, and I pray they may believe in the ways of the Lord. For it is written, "My people perish for lack of knowledge" and "Where no counsel is, the people fall, but in the multitude of counselors there is safety." I am but a counselor and a messenger in the name of Jesus.

The following articles are four statements of "prophetic utterance" to the church and for the church, but not necessarily by the church but by the Spirit. I appeal to one and to all to consider these words that they might be profitable to your ministry. The following is a short synopsis of each:

The first, "The Declaration of the Mystery of the Last Days," reveals the mystery of God unfolding in end times as the Scripture states. It announces to the Church to prepare for final deliverance from judgment. In addition, it issues a warning to an unbelieving world concerning His prophetic word on the Jews' return as a nation, thereby proving the reality of His Word on earth. Finally, it also declares to Israel a deliverance to come despite their unbelief in Jesus as we see now. God is going to show to the world that His love will be the greater. He will deliver Israel at last and yet judge a world that rejects His grace.

The second and third statements of utterance speak specifically to America, God's country as we have declared it. America has become a place full of disobedience to the laws of God, and even the churches seek to justify their own sins, bringing to life the words of the apostle Paul, which read, "Let no man deceive you by any means: For that shall not come, except there come a falling away first, and that man of sin shall be revealed, the son of perdition" (2 Thessalonians 2:3). Five of the seven letters addressed to the churches in the Book of Revelations chapters two through four reveal a sad conclusion—Jesus admires their works but declares they have forgotten their first love...Him. He requests of them to repent. Clearly in America, our churches, consisting of many denominations and cultures, are failing to sustain pure and sound biblical doctrine. With true repentance before our God being practically nonexistent among much of the Christian community, many members come to church but fail to come to Christ. As the institution of Christianity weakens, so shall America the nation.

The fourth statement is a word concerning God's righteous judgment. In essence, would it be fair to try only Israel by Christ's first coming and not also try every other nation by his second coming? As Christ tested Israel, the Holy Spirit has allowed me to see how God is using Israel to test the world to see if the Gentiles believe the word concerning Israel's return as Israel was required to believe the prophetic word concerning who Jesus Christ was. I declare that our religiosity is doing the same thing to us as it did to Israel. The question I ask is, could we reject within our hearts the reality of Israel's salvation, fulfilling Scripture at last? Would not this act restore and prove absolute truth to the glory of God and no one else? Could God be showing the world what truth is and where it sits (inside the gates of Jerusalem when the battle rages in the Valley of Jehoshaphat on the other side of that gate)?

We, the church, ought to be saying what a mighty God we serve as this reality nears with each passing day. God's Word warns us in Romans 11 not to be boastful, envious, or jealous in that day but to prepare to see righteousness about to be performed when Zion the Deliverer comes. The fourth statement addresses these concerns because I see so many sleeping saints in churches across America and the time is short. When the preacher of righteousness speaks, he is usually called directly by God to declare it, and I sense it to be the final call, even the last resort.

Do come that we may have eyes that we may see and ears that we may hear, that a rejoicing may begin within our hearts, and that the promotion of the Gospel might reach out to a lost world one more time. The Spirit of Truth shall declare His story through the prophets of the Lord in the hour that God Himself determines it. And let our hearts know it is only fair that if first the Jew, now the Gentile, and this is the Lord's righteousness that He is set to perform! I hope the following four statements of prophetic utterance add knowledge and wisdom, giving the church clarity, and all of which belongs to the glory of God. I am but a cry in the wilderness!

Purpose: For the Perfecting of the Saints

Ephesians 4:11–13

"Utterance in the year of 1995"

THE DECLARATION OF THE MYSTERY OF THE LAST DAYS
Written July 1991

THE LORD GOD WHOM WE serve... is a living God
full of grace and tender mercies

Oh, but is His anger to be kindled

And His heart to take offense in that great and notable day!

Let us hear His justice that we might know our sins.

Has not His Son been falsely accused?

Oh, do man quest for that which is right... all men!

Yet he sees not the injustice against one found even without sin.

For the Lord has published it before all the peoples of the earth.

But their ears are plugged and eyes are shut.

Righteousness to them is only for them indeed.

How foolish is thee who questions not!

That no answer can I give when no question is asked.

Thou runneth from me, oh man, running into mine adversary.

For remember, there is an enemy in the path.

And his time draweth near and his kingdom is fallen.

And so shall the kingdoms of yours, oh man, do likewise.

Shall you not be full of anger... full of desperate lies when I, even I, the Lord, say enough!

Thou shalt know it most assuredly.

By the mouth of my own prophets shall thou know it.

Rise up, my Church, and hear them well.

For I have come unto you to speak as I have to my own nation.

The earth is thine wilderness

And the New Jerusalem shall come down upon it.

So shall my prophets prophesy concerning Jerusalem.

For it is full of strife, full of division, and is now the blood beginning to flow as I knew it would.

For there are giants in the land, my Church

But do remember the report of Joshua and Caleb.

For they believed by faith and were rewarded and so must you!

Oh, my prophets, do look upon Israel the nation

Lest I send prophets from Israel the nation.

Church, do consider this ancient nation in these modern times.

For it is my written word moving before all the earth.

Has it not been spoken from days long gone.

And yet I am refused! But I AM THAT I AM... as then

And with a great thunder, I AM THAT I AM... even now!

My people are few in the midst of many.

Is it not for a demonstration?

Remember by my ancient prophets did I not speak

That I do this not for their sake but for my namesake!

For my nation is full of pride and indeed boastful.

But what of you, Brazil, and what of you, Iran and Italy and China and Russia and Nigeria and oh, so many other nations.

I ask do you serve me… Do you declare my Son?

And do I have tears for my America… tears indeed!

You have refused to hear my trumpets as Israel refused in the wilderness.

Come ye out of her, my saints… for she is fallen! She is fallen!

Therefore, publish this before the congregation,

That they might know, oh man.

For to know me is to hear me… Such is My righteousness.

So hear this and hear this well… for the words are a certainty.

Ask the Lord again the question,

"Will thou at this time restore again the kingdom to Israel?" as it is written.

Ask indeed, my Israel.

That I might provide the answer!

For thus saith the Lord concerning the question.

This is how I shall put all things under the feet of my Son.

I shall permit a weight to come upon the backs of Israel

And they shall be heavy laden with burdens.

And you, oh Gentiles, shall perform it so!

You shall serve me well in your unbelief concerning my Word

And Israel shall cry out when all the world is encamped around thee.

When their politics, their armor, their economies, and even their gods

Shall seek to bring my nation to its end.

Shall then my nation say, "Come, my Lord, do Come!"

Can they repent?

Will I yet cast away their transgression against me?

Does not my Word declare that salvation shall rest in Me?

So shall it be! For there will be no other nation, people, weapon, or hope

That can save thee but by Him that was rejected.

Is it not written by my prophet Zechariah

"Then shall the Lord go forth, and fight against those nations,

As when he fought in the day of battle.

And His feet shall stand in that Day upon the Mount of Olives, which is before Jerusalem."

I ask what other god can declare such a purpose?

And make known such a mystery that is before all the earth!

How precious is the work of mine own Son... Savior to the Gentiles.

And shall I also demonstrate... Messiah to the Jews!

I declare to all those who have an ear, it is not the Church or Israel

But the Church and Israel!

And by my Son shall they both be one new man.

And then the Scripture shall be fulfilled as written in Romans 11:15

"For if the casting away of them be the reconciling of the world,

What shall the receiving of them be but, life from the dead."

And therein shall the Lord God be glorified

And all the earth shall see it and know it.

Oh indeed, How sweet the grace of God.

Who can measure His grace and who can perform His mercy!

Beware, Gentiles. Prepare my Church for that great and notable day is now.

Behold, I will make all things new in that hour as promised to those who believe.

For the earnest expectation is indeed the blessed hope.

Look up, the Lord declares, I say look up for the visitation!

Thus has the Lord written. So shall my prophets declare it!

TEARS FOR AMERICA

OH LAND… FAR FROM THE Apple of my Eye

Great has been thy calling… A place of refuge for the many.

Some out of necessity and some by the yoke.

Yet has not all been blessed in its Promise?

Did not we put our Hope in thee… the Lord!

Despite the error of our ways, we stood corrected

And blessed in His knowledge none the same.

Many indeed, yes, many a seed among men.

Having the same dreams… the same hope… and the same God.

Blessed were we as the Lord smiled upon us as we sought Him out.

But oh, America… Where are thee now? Cannot the Lord ask?

And can we answer the question while we are caught up in the Fruits
provided and hearing not His Voice?

Do the children know His ways for to tell their own?

I think not!

Mighty America, everyone in you cries for things to be their way.

There is no contentment, and where is the unity?

They cry not for the Lord anymore for they know Him not!

Oh, America… an arm of support to my chosen, are you compromis-
ing In your success?

In the name of democracy you gained freedom.

But was not your freedom founded on Truth!

Therefore, are you not being swallowed up in your own design?

Yes… diversity being your promise can also become your curse!

Where is the truth when you honor

The lies of those afar in your politeness?

Oh, America… Have you not abandoned your own children

Preferring to court the favors of outsiders for the few inside?

How long, land of the free? How long, land of the free?

We are burdened by our greed… Enslaved by debt of our choosing!

With our God we are neither hot nor cold but lukewarm…

Giving in without giving our all, only to give up!

Therefore, I have Tears for my America.

Yes… the hope of the world has been in thee.

And I can see none finer in the Lord than America.

Therefore, I have Tears for the World also.

For when America speaks no more for the True God…

Then the True God must speak for Himself,

And then there shall be tears in America… Tears indeed!

Thus the Lord do Saith… Amen and Amen.

And it is written concerning he who prophesies:

"And if thou say in thine heart,

How shall we know the word which the Lord hath not spoken?

When a prophet speaks in the name of the Lord,

If the thing follow not, nor come to pass,

That is the thing which the Lord hath not spoken,

But the prophet has spoken presumptuously:

Therefore, thou shalt not be afraid of him" (Deuteronomy 18:21-22).

"For Jesus Himself testified, that a prophet hath no honor in his own country" (John 4:44).

"Behold, I have told you before!" (Matthew 24:25).

Purpose: For the work of the ministry
Ephesians 4:11–13
"To prepare the saints"

AN ANSWER TO THE TEARS...MY AMERICA!

Written on April 28, 1995
A response to America's memorial service
for the Oklahoma bombing tragedy

I HAVE HEARD THE CRY of my countrymen. I have seen the tears of the daughters of thine nation. And now do we lift up our voices in anxious prayer! Now do we seek His refuge and search Him out! And He has heard our cry, but He returned unto me a question. For the Lord does ask, "What is it that we require?" And we do answer for ourselves. We shall overcome! Singing "God Bless America" as if He is ours and ours alone, do we examine ourselves that we might wonder? I think not! Indeed, our hearts act above reproach. And even our courts are in disarray, believing our rights to be above His laws.

He asks, "Are we the better for it?" Oh, what a wretched nation we have become! Even our adversaries are beginning to know justice better than we do. And they are now set to look upon our calamity. Oh, America! For our democracy has blinded us, and we have backslidden in our freedom. And the Lord does ask me, His servant among servants, "How much freedom shall we require with our democracy?" Shall your purpose be for an occasion to sin? But because His grace is so abundant, we are certain to misappropriate it in our freedom for He is mindful of our policies on Capitol Hill, and our amendments from place to place are indeed contrary to Him. Indeed, we are in opposition to His very laws. But He is God, and He states, "I change not!"

Is it not peculiar that the name of Him whom the Lord has christened is silenced even within our institutions of learning? And even now we begin to suffer loss, not just in the heartland of our nation but from coast to coast. Listen up, for even the beauty of America has become tarnished! The Lord has rained a cleansing, but we are refusing a refreshing. I assure you we have not met His wrath, but by His chastening, we will learn from the absence of His grace, for the elements of the earth shall consume us in our disobedience.

Think, oh man. The Lord requires you to hear. Why, oh Gentiles, can't you rejoice in the salvation of Israel? Have you not profited from their fall as an object lesson? Is not the very works of His hand made known to us through Israel? And now it is before us night and day for an understanding and as evidence. But knowledge we have refused, and wisdom we do cast out! Oh, but the Lord has placed a hot word upon my lips. He has lit a fire within my heart!

Requiring a proclamation, He says, Oh man, loose the cause of Israel before their faces even before the earth. And make known the purpose of the Lord before the congregation. Establish the God of Israel for a demonstration of His power and His glory, for He is set once again to restore the Tabernacle of David before their eyes. And the Lord knows that you shall be jealous in His sight, ye Gentiles. Our concerns will be in opposition to His agenda, which shall be *by the Word*. Let us turn our attention to truth that we might see His justice set against the nations who are contrary to His nation and His Son. Is this not but the very display of His mercy to those nations throughout the ages?

We are in attendance in the court of our God and know our sins. Therefore, the Lord has proven our guilt through the innocence of His Son. I say, make way, for justice shall be served to the transgressors against truth and promise. Harden not your hearts against the knowing of His ways. It is a truth that the Lord has caused me to speak. May the people of God hear these words for this is the conclusion of the matter. The Lord has a concern above our own, America! How many of you remember that we serve the God of Israel? Can we bear it that we might gain from it? I pray the saints do accept it in humility. Which gospel do we serve the Lord asks—to promote Him or to protect ourselves?

Church, I appeal to you to hear this line of thought, which comes by the Spirit. Satan blinded Israel through their selfishness, and so they did stumble. Is he blinding even the saints that they might stumble over the Word concerning Israel? I affirm that our indifference has become equivalent to Israel's. Was not the Word written concerning Jesus, and Israel refused to believe in that hour? Now the Word is written concerning Israel's return, and we do not consider it in our hour!

As Israel rejected the Christ in their ignorance, I have been made to see also that the church institution is in unbelief concerning the Hope of Israel's salvation. Oh, the wisdom of the Lord in the performing of His test. What goes around has indeed come around! And I cannot refuse it or argue its point. This is righteousness at its finest, and I know God is the preparer of it. Church of Gentiles, be careful of having your own righteousness. Be careful indeed, for God is not subordinate to your thoughts nor your traditions but requires our obedience to His thoughts, lest we fail also.

Therefore, do not dismay but prepare for instruction. The Lord has set before Him a new voice and given unto those a vision. And I do see an ancient promise set to be fulfilled, and it is a revelation. The Lord did state, "I will pour out my Spirit and they shall prophesy of it." Indeed the time has come for the *Anointed One*. Remember, is not the time an appointed end to this world that another might come? I forewarn that you do not forget the Lord's covenant with Israel or shall you refuse to remember it being wise in your own conceit? It can be counted against you in the day the Lord should you be required to believe it.

Therefore, this is my answer to your tears, oh America. "As you choose to cast my Son from your democracy that other religions may abide, as you choose to make acceptable before Me man with man and woman with woman, as your politics approves gambling and your credit approves debt, so shall I permit it that you may fall from the weight of your greed in your freedom. For it shall be a curse to you, and I shall sit back, and your cries I shall not hear. Then the Lord you shall be without, and in your diversity, there will be calamity."

But to my Church, remember the Lord's decree of faith. Remember the prophecy that must yet be fulfilled by the Word, for it is a more sure word. Remember thy first love and His kingdom that is to come. Remember the judgment, which must be served through the revelation of His Son. Remember His promise to Israel, for He will covet them in that hour. Are not all these things written in the same Book for remembrance? Reality is about to check in upon the earth, and there is no excuse for not seeing that which can be seen and read and understood for the glory of God and His truth. I pray thee judge not according to appearance but judge with righteous judgment. Let us not say no to His Word for it is the name of Jesus. And is it already written? Prepare the saints to wear robes of righteousness for there is a wedding to attend. Rejoice now. I say, rejoice evermore in this truth, for by the grace of God do I bring you a minority report as did Joshua and Caleb. And how few did follow them, for there was not one. Christ is before us; let us Hear Him for He states, "Behold, I have told you before."

But who shall love truth that they might desire righteousness be served? Our God has been merciful and full of patience that we should know His grace indeed. I commission your prayers for a prophet of the Lord has no honor...yet! And who shall believe such a report in the time that it should be known? But the righteousness of the Lord is my strength, and He shall be my shield, for the Lord loves the righteous one. So be ye righteous by wisdom, my Church. Wisdom does cry out into the streets and whispers gently before the saints. Where is righteousness that it might be performed? I thank God that His Word has been placed before us to know Him. For the Word states, "Through knowledge are the righteous delivered." Let us speak with unspeakable joy that a real kingdom draws near for a silent thunder is set to roar, and the earth will be shaken!

In closing, I say, open thine heart to the seeing of His ways, and thou shalt be with Jesus, for it is good that the Bride should know the coming of her Groom, that the wedding might be pure and holy. Come, the Lord does say. Come, indeed! Even if need be, repent that ye may come before Him. Come one and come all and be ye forgiven. Amen and amen!

Purpose: For the Perfecting of the Saints
Ephesians 4:11–13

IN ALL FAIRNESS, SUCH IS THE LORD'S RIGHTEOUSNESS

HEAR, EARTH, AND ALL ITS inhabitants, the Word of the Lord for the time has come, and the moment has already been declared. But the people go about their way, unaware and so unconcerned, consumed in the serving of themselves, for themselves, night and day. They continuously gather only to be found without what they really need. Be still, those who are quick upon the earth, that you might hear. Be observant that you might see and come to know. For the time of the Lord's visitation draws near indeed. Now that the earth is full of the abundance of men and their inventions, what shall man conquer next that he can overcome by his own strength? By our intellect we have stood upon the moon and searched the very heavens for our comparison and have found none. But that does not mean that there are none to be considered.

The Word of God sits upon our shelves that we might hear "*Thus saith the Lord!*" But man rejects the God that is for the god he wants, much to his own hurt. The Word of God has withstood time itself and has overcome the unbelief of those who choose unbelief. It has endured and continuously persevered throughout the ages, penned by His servants of the ancient days. Is not the Word even before you and I? Indeed, even the Word has overcome the judgment of the Tower of Babel. It has risen even above His stumbling nation to show the Lord stumbles not. Though He scattered those at the Tower of Babel, did He not also bring man back together at Pentecost? How marvelous is the Lord! Has not the Lord translated His Word that the many tongues might receive it? For in this generation, who cannot have it before him? Which one of us can give a worthy excuse of ignorance before the God of Israel? For the Spirit has published His Word and set forth His works, promoting it to the ends of the earth as the Lord said must be done…first!

And so has He performed it, for indeed no weapon has prospered against Him. Now can all the earth make a decision, yes, even a firm rejection? And can the whole earth not do it universally, collectively, and conclusively? This is the wisdom of the Lord and the patience of His grace—He waits! And has not our God also waited for man but to no avail? So many of us have gone astray and now even refuse to turn from sin. We have an excuse for every wrong and a blame for every fault. But where is our own account, and can it be hidden from God?

There is a thorn that God Himself has placed in the midst of the earth. And that old devil called Satan fights against the Word of God by blinding the world to His Word, and oh, what a multitude He has. For what ought to be a rose before the church has the appearance of a thorn to the earth. And the church is also ready to see it as a thorn, except those who walk by the Word. And the Word is by the Spirit, and the Holy Spirit giveth us the wisdom of Christ. And His wisdom dictates a thorny issue, which shall determine true faith. That thorn is Israel, which shall be His rod of tension in the midst, a great time of decision for the whole world that they might believe in Jesus. It shall cause a trembling among the nations who have not His Word in the presence of their people nor his hope in the depths of their hearts.

Is He not a God who can choose and yet deny, give grace and yet perform a test? Who can announce in ancient times things that are to be in the end times? Oh man, look and give reverence unto the Lord. What a merciful God we serve, for Israel shall be His sign upon the earth, a sign that shall be refused and is refused because the Lord shall be refused. But He is the Holy God who owns justice and is entitled to perform it against all who walk in unbelief. We serve a crucified Savior who owns the right of retribution. Oh Earth, take heed and study for He does require of His people that they might know Him.

How does the Lord try the nations like Israel the nation was tried? Why should Israel be the only nation to be measured against His Law and truth? Listen up, ye nations, for the Lord is also set to try you as He did Israel! All ye Gentiles of the many nations, the Lord stands before us all by the Word through the rebirth of His nation as Christ stood before them in His birth. Christ fulfilled the Scriptures literally that the reality of God might be known to us, but at whose expense, Church? Whose stumbling caused you to be lifted up? Whose ignorance of the Lord was made public that the Gentiles would profit from? It is the power of God under demonstration through His nation that gave us His truth, giving us our salvation and our redemption and our hope even to be resurrected! Oh, He has given a stunning revelation for the time of the end, and I do fall upon my face. Praise God from whom all knowledge flows that we might have wisdom from Him.

We ought to love Israel for the burden they were made to bear, for we have gained! I forewarn you of this with deep mourning. Israel is the root, and we are branches. We cannot separate ourselves from this truth, or surely we shall stumble also. Oh Israel, cry out to the crucified One that He might prove His resurrection, and by your repentance surely He must come for His Word promises us all. And now Israel is fulfilling the Word unaware to make known the reality of who God is before those who choose to deny the cross of Jesus and the redemption of Israel. I have found that Angel of Light who deceiveth the whole world. Church, none of our goodness shall prevail against the deceiver of this kind. But truth and only truth will stand that God Himself may be glorified in righteousness. Will the real Israel please stand up? Is the church Israel or is Israel… Israel? Cannot God have two vessels of His making, or will man deny God the privilege only to lose due to his own selfishness? This I forewarn to all.

Satan whispers, "Did God really say He would restore Israel?" I proclaim emphatically by the Word that it states Yes…Yes…and Yes! God is indeed standing the nation up, and the world refuses to believe. Even the churches contend with God and consider it not. Therefore, whose side are we really on, Church? The Word or the world? Shall it be what we think, or shall it be what actually can be seen and yet we refuse? Yes, what a mighty God we serve. For the Word does state: "Let every man be a liar that God may be true" and it will be so in the hour that He demonstrates it.

I am commanded to write the vision and stand in the gap as a cry in the wilderness, for the battle is set in the Valley of Jehoshaphat, and Jerusalem is God's place of visit. He will not be denied in that final hour. It will be His moment in time. God's thoughts indeed are higher than our thoughts, as high as the heavens above earth. Fear the Lord God and judge not, for the law of man is no better than the heart of the man. But the Law of God brings long life to those who follow it. And the Law of Christ even saves the soul for eternal blessings!

So hear this as I close. Ask God the question that He awaits—Why is Israel back? Let the Church pray this before the throne of God. And I heard His answer in the depths of my spirit as it was declared. Thus saith the Lord by the Spirit of Truth, righteousness means "in all fairness." Can the Lord stand before one nation only and require they know Him and not also require from all other nations that they know Him as well by test? In all fairness, Israel had to believe in Christ's first coming.

Would it be right not to try the Gentiles' belief in His second coming? Read the Book to see!

In all fairness, people of the earth, don't you want equal opportunity also? So shall it be that the nations shall have their trial as Israel did that righteousness might be performed and justice can be served to those who make the same error and have even a lesser excuse than Israel, for they are an example. Remember, except when our righteousness exceeds the righteousness of the Pharisee, we will not see any better than they did. Let the Black man see only black, and the White man see only white. And every kind shall see it their way! For every man shall take hold of his tradition at the expense of losing Christ. The Lord states, "For My Word is not in you that you might believe in Me only." As the Jew, so shall be the Gentile. The Lord God does try the heart!

I prophesy to you this—as Jesus was nailed to the cross, so is Israel to be nailed by a world of unbelief. And this time the Lord Himself shall answer Israel's cry, and the True God shall be made known. To dust shall all the religions of this world crumble, even the denominations! But not the Word and neither the believer that overcomes by faith in Jesus's name. This is the work of our gospel in this generation. Be ye not afraid! This is the seal which the Lord has graced me to open and to see by

His Word. This is the prophecy that now must come, and God Himself shall no more be seen darkly through obscure glass but as clear as crystal in pure righteousness. And the prophecy of the Seventieth Week of Daniel will sum up all things as written. For the woman and her man child is Israel and the Lord Jesus. And the rejected Son will yet be received by the nation to the glory of God. As Savior to the Gentiles, let the Lord demonstrate also Messiah to the Jews! Let all men take their places and declare before God where ye stand. For the deliverance has come that the world will know what a mighty God we serve!

A LETTER OF EXPLANATION

I ALWAYS THOUGHT OF THE Book of Revelation as one huge chaotic battle. I could not determine who was fighting who and why. I also found it difficult to grasp how the whole world could be in error and ultimately condemned, either by God or by man himself. These thoughts led me to ask the question "How could man be so wrong and God be so right that such a book had to be written?"

In the middle of my searching for the answer, the nation of Israel kept coming into view. And so I considered a second question "What is the meaning of Israel's rebirth of May 1948 and does it have any pro- phetic significance?" At this point in time, an answer has been provided, and my search is finished. Without question, I desire all to know what I have come to know. I realized this compassion as the Spirit revealed His truths so clearly and consistently. And so I was directed to write so that I might better reveal to those a perspective not being given proper attention. For the Spirit of Truth states "That if it is given to me to know, then it is by faith my responsibility to reveal." The Spirit only speaks God's perspective. To date, I have written three "Articles of Divine Revelation." They are:

- "The Necessity of the Return of God's Chosen People," dated 16 May 1990
- "Prophecy is Alive and Well, and Israel is the Key," dated 22 November 1990
- "The Paradox of the Seventieth Week of Daniel," dated 3 April 1991

It is felt that these inspired letters could add tremendously to the edification of the church concerning events in the decade of the 1990s. I am honored that the Lord has placed them in my possession, and I give my praise continuously to Him. Therefore I conclude on the matter, for I feel the most difficult and yet the most inspiring has been accomplished. It is a most refreshing thought to know that there will be a truly "everlasting righteousness," an "end to sins," and a very real "eternal life." Yes, man has a God who blessed him with so much more, and yet will He do so again.

Let us covet truth perhaps more than anything else, for it is written "that some perish due to lack of knowledge." Yes, I am issuing a stern warning to all. Unbeknown to me at the time of the writing of my articles (1990s and beyond) was the recurring statement of "Be fore-warned!!!" I do believe in a pre-tribulation rapture, but that does not mean we will not be tried as the hour approaches. The real question is: Do you believe in religion more than truth?

I have attempted to explain the things we do see first! I believe that if we can understand Israel's rebirth and that it is God's calling, then we are in a much better frame of mind to believe what is yet to come. I know many will fall because of their unwillingness to consider God's perspective, thinking themselves right in their own eyes. It has happened so many times in history's past, yet man still has not learned. There is no excuse. The sin, in this case, is simply self-righteousness, better known as pride. Man is full of pride. Therefore, prepare to do without it, for it is written in Proverbs 16:18 "Pride goeth before destruction, and an haughty spirit before a fall."

I now look forward, desiring to add clarity to many points of interest concerning "prophetic structure" of future events. The task is very challenging, but I do not take God's Word in vain. If He thought it best to be written, let us think it best to be read. I will highlight a basic framework of key events to be fulfilled.

I don't have all the answers, and I know it is probably best no one does. But I am moved by the advice the Scriptures give to one and to all—"Brethren, if any of you do err from the truth, and one convert him; Let him know, that he which converteth the sinner from the error of his way shall save a soul from death, and shall hide a multitude of sins" (James 5:19–20). This is my mission, a prophet's mission, if you will. If God is eternal, then why can't we be also? And if heaven is real, then hell must be as real. So I speak as a prophet—the Word of the Lord is truth! And here is wisdom: When man abandons God, God shall abandon man, and man in his unbelief shall fall prey to his own works of destruction.

The basic prophetic structure is:

1. The Beast and the Ten-Horned Kingdom
2. Mystery Babylon and Literal Babylon
3. The Church of Christ and the Tribulation Saints
4. Israel's Redemption Promised and the Millennial Kingdom
5. Jesus, The Spirit of Prophecy,…is the Final Word!
   Note: Each subject will be addressed later.

The primary purpose is to reflect the following:

- Combine related Scripture,
- Show how Scripture defines Scripture,
- Give an awareness of time, and
- Format to aid in instructing others

Gregory A. Booker, finis

LETTER IV

Inspired 17 April 1991

Ten-Horned Kingdom Led by the Antichrist

The Mysteries of the Book of Daniel

THE PURPOSE OF THE BOOK of Daniel is to detail the prophecies of the Gentile world kingdoms from Daniel's day to the millennium and eternal kingdom of God on Earth. It was written approximately 616 to 535 BC and authored by Daniel, a captive prince from Judah. Daniel served as a prime minister under several kings and was gifted as an interpreter of dreams and visions. And he served as a prophet of the Lord.

THE MAN OF METALS

DANIEL 2

- Verses 31 to 33—Kingdoms described as "The Man of Metals" (my designation)
- Verses 34 to 35—"A stone was cut out without hands" (This is Jesus!)
- Verses 36 to 43—An interpretation of the Man of Metals

OBSERVATIONS

The head of gold portion of the great image represented the first of five kingdoms in the vision. Babylon had Israel in captivity for a period of seventy years at the time of the vision.

The breast and arms of the image symbolize the Medo-Persian Kingdom which succeeded Babylon at the end of the seventy years captivity. The two arms symbolize the two nations, the Medes and the Persians. The Medo-Persian Kingdom was inferior to the Babylonian Empire as silver is to gold.

The belly and the thighs symbolize the Grecian Empire. (Additional prophetic information is discussed in chapter eight of Daniel.)

The leg of iron image symbolizes the Roman Empire which followed Greece in the domination of Israel. This kingdom was to be stronger than all the preceding kingdoms as iron is stronger than gold, silver, and brass. The two legs of iron represent the eastern and western divisions of the old Roman Empire due to its vastness.

The feet and the toes of iron and clay represent the future revised Roman Empire, the fifth kingdom in the image to oppress Israel in the "times of the Gentiles." As the last part of the image, it will be destroyed by the "stone" from heaven. Being part iron indicates a revived Roman Empire. The ten toes represent the ten nations that will exist in the last days before Christ's return.

The "stone" that smote the image symbolizes the kingdom of heaven, headed by the Lord Jesus Christ, at his Second coming, destroying the kingdoms of the current world system.

KINGDOMS DESCRIBED AS SYMBOLIC ANIMALS: DANIEL 7:1–8

The king of Babylon was symbolized by the lion (Isaiah 5:29). The eagle's wings also identify Babylon for it is compared to an eagle (Jeremiah 48:40). The lion denotes regalness, and the eagle swiftness for its conquests over its enemies. The second kingdom, which was like a bear, was the Medo-Persian Empire. The bear is a fitting symbol because of its cruelty, thirst for blood, robberies, and love of spoils (Isaiah 13:16–18). Also, the largest species of bear is found in the mountains of Media. The Babylonian Empire was conquered by the Medes and Persians about 530 BC when they ingeniously built a dam in the Euphrates River.

The leopard is a fitting symbol of the Grecian Empire founded by Alexander the Great. This animal is known for its quickness. This together with the four wings of a fowl denotes the double swiftness of conquests even over Babylon. The Greeks conquered the Persian empire in 331 BC. Verse 6 continues with "the beast had also four heads" as predicted in Daniel 8, the Greek Empire disintegrated when the first king, Alexander, died prematurely. The prediction of the "four heads" came true when four powers from within divided the kingdom into four lesser kingdoms. Daniel 8 reveals where the Antichrist will come from.

And behold a fourth beast, dreadful and terrible, and it had ten horns, and there came up among them another little horn. Verses 7 and 8 are the first signs of a kingdom which has not yet come.

POINTS OF INTEREST

- It is fascinating that Daniel wrote about events he himself did not know or have anything to do with in their later fulfillment. The time span of events alone, not including the ten horns, covers over five hundred years. It would be wise to conclude that if God can predict or perhaps "administer" five hundred years (Babylon thru Roman Empire), God can predict two thousand years.
- It is easy to see why Daniel was so grieved at the visions, for these beast all had one common factor. They were Gentile nations that had dominion over Israel as history has indeed proven. Why are there two different symbolic pictures to describe the same na-

tions? Perhaps it is to add greater clarity to who the nations are and to also emphasize their power and notably to provide more information on the Greeks and the ten horns.

- Notice also that the fourth kingdom of the metals, Rome, is not mentioned in the kingdoms of animals. Why? The "kingdom of animals" represents each kingdom at the height of its power. As great as old Rome was, it will be even greater near the end times. The iron legs which continue in the feet denotes a Roman presence that will sustain itself. And so it has. Over two thousand years later, Roman culture is known and even respected worldwide. There is a revised Roman kingdom yet to come.

- All the previous kingdoms dominated Israel but could not destroy it. If the pattern is to continue, Israel must exist as a nation once again if a valid domination is to occur. And so it does now. We are all familiar with the European Common Market—it is the iron of the feet, but who is the clay? Time will tell.

FOUR HORNS REVEALED

DANIEL 8

The Ram (Medo-Persia) and The He-Goat (Greek)

A vision is given of the ram and the he-goat in Daniel 8:1–14 before its interpretation. In verse 16, the angel Gabriel is told to make Daniel understand the vision he saw. Daniel is also told "at the time appointed, the end shall be."

The interpreter identifies the he-goat as Grecia, and as we know, four kingdoms did stand up out of the nation. Verse 23 states "and in the latter time of their kingdom, when the transgressors are come to full," and it implies that these nations will stay in existence until they reach their full power. Who are these nations? History gives the answer, or better yet, an encyclopedia will do wonders! The four nations who at one time were representative of the Grecian Empire are today known as the following: Egypt, Syria, Turkey, and Greece.

Verse 23 continues with "a king of fierce countenance…shall stand up." This is information about the Antichrist! At this point, all we know is that he will come from one of these nations. Their profiles:

- Egypt—an Arab nation; religion is Islam

- Syria—an Arab nation; religion is Islam
- Turkey—Arab/Europe mix; religion is Islamic
- Greece—European mix; religion is Greek Orthodox Church (Eastern is separate from the Roman Catholic and Protestant churches); also Muslims are the largest religious minority.

Regarding the current political setup of the European Common Market (ECM), Greece is a full fledge member and has been for some time, and Turkey has requested membership recently, but its status is pending. The ECM has given arguments opposing Turkey's application. I believe there are ulterior motives for ECM hesitancy (for example, different racial type, different religion (Islamic), adverse form of government) that could explain their reluctance, though they may not admit it.

At this point I would like to address the issue of the best prophetic Scripture for where the Antichrist will come from:

Daniel 11 deals prophetically with the future of the division of Greece into four kingdoms. It highlights the battles of war between "king of the north" which is Syria and "king of the south" which is Egypt. The series of conflict between these two nations began to fulfill Scripture primarily around 200 BC. Verse 31 reveals an act of abomination of desolation which was performed by Antiochus Epiphanes, a Syrian king. He hated the Jews and desecrated the Jewish temple by slaughtering a pig in the holy of holies in approximately 165 BC.

Now notice verse 35 where it jumps forward to the "time of the end." However, the reference to the kings of the north and the south continue in verse 40. Also verses 36–39 clearly reveal the personality of the Antichrist. Verses 40–43 detail the conquest of which of the two nations? It is the king of the north who is pushed and then becomes the aggressor. The victorious one is none other than Syria. Therefore, the victorious nation must also be the nation led by none other than the Antichrist...Bravo!

Now further conclusions can be made by this discovery. Can we say he shall be Arab? Can we also say that the best candidate to sign an effective peace treaty with Israel is the one who fights against Israel the most—Syria? It seems quite remote that Syria and Egypt could be full members of the ECM. They are as different as people could be. Something dramatic would have to happen, and between the two, Syria, due to its terrorist label, seems impossible as a welcomed member. This distinction is a critical point to consider of which I will deal with later.

I detailed all this to perhaps lead us to a peculiar observation. And that is this—could a scenario present a situation for the Arabs that due to their logistics, sympathy (because of Desert Storm), increased military strength, political fairness for a New World Order, and of course, oil for economic stability, that they are indeed accepted? Furthermore, could the Arabs be the clay? Clay is flexible but weak.

THE PROPHETIC PROGRESSION OF THE TEN-HORNED KINGDOM

DANIEL 7:15–28

At this point we have seen Scripture predicting the Ten-Horned Kingdom, identification of four of the ten horns, the revealing of where the Antichrist shall come from, and most notably, have gained confidence in the power of God's Prophetic Word concerning prior fulfillment of the past kingdoms. In retrospect, one should ask the question "Who benefits most from these prophetic revelations?" It certainly does not do the prior empires much good. However, let it be said that we would need the future to occur in order to decode the past. In other words, it is the future itself that unlocks the key to His plan. Relish that thought for a moment and you have just a glimpse of His power! Let us continue to pursue the prophetic word.

Daniel 7:24 states, "And the ten horns out of this kingdom are ten kings that shall arise: and another shall rise after them; and he shall be diverse from the first, and he shall subdue three kings." The general consensus is that all four horns will be part of the ten horns before the Antichrist arrives. Though I don't deny the possibility, there is the chance of a slightly different scenario. I believe that only three of the revealed horns will be accepted by the ECM. Those three nations are Egypt, Turkey, and Greece.

We must remember the Antichrist will sign a treaty with Israel. Israel has little to do with the ten-horned entity until after the Beast (Antichrist) gains control of the kingdom. Therefore, there is a real potential for a peace treaty to be signed independent of ECM. Strong undercurrents are already supporting Syria as an Arab leader nation in negotiating peace with Israel. However, the Beast will not arrive on the scene until the Ten-Horned Kingdom comes into existence. Each force is independent until the Beast overcomes three of the horns, thereby forcing the others to give him their power also. Syria's terrorist label and their aggressive past supports this observation.

Another point of interest is that the current ECM has many more nations (twelve) than the future ECM I have predicted. If four of the horns being revealed are Arab nations, the ECM will only have six or, at the most, seven nations representing a "revived Roman empire." Wisdom dictates that there will be a tremendous change in world government of a magnitude never before seen. The Lord is showing those who dare to consider His Word in operation, and it is to His glory and His power that these things can be known.

We must recognize and accept the potential for change and the tensions that shall erupt due to those changes. For example, The United States and Soviet Union are both desperately hanging on to "old politics" tactics. They have dominated world opinion for almost fifty years and are now "both at the same time" in serious distress. Operation Desert Storm accelerated the USA's vulnerability and, in a strange way, brought a divided world together almost begging for a New World Order. In addition, the USSR's newly formed republics, Europe's restructuring to facilitate single government policy, including Germany's resurgence, and just worldwide civil unrest are creating eerie and endless possibilities. And there is always the potential for consolidation due to desperation. Look at all the mega mergers going on in America. I sense a similar phenomenon nation to nation. The world is entering the stage of the unknown and much must still occur before the Beast is even revealed.

Daniel 11:35–45 gives greater detail about the conquest of the Beast, which includes him conquering even more countries. Michael, the archangel, is the prince who defends Israel in the angelic realm. I no longer doubt this, for there must be some force which orchestrates accurate fulfillment of prophecy. Daniel 10 further reveals—to those who dare believe—the angelic realm at war. This concludes references of the ten horns in the Book of Daniel.

THE MYSTERIES OF THE BOOK OF REVELATIONS CONCERNING THE BEAST AND THE TEN-HORNED KINGDOM

REVELATIONS 10:1–11 PROVIDES MORE INFORMATION on the Beast and his kingdom in addition to what we already know—ten horns support-ed by seven heads. Notice that verse 2 references the same symbolic figure found in the Book of Daniel. (Marvel at the fact that over six hundred years separated these two books and Israel the nation was under very different conditions.) Much of Revelation 13:18 is self-explanatory; however, notice what happens in verse 11. It states "And I beheld another beast coming up out of the earth; and he had two horns like a lamb." Could this be referring to the False Prophet of Isra-el—Israel's false messiah? The "Lamb" has always referred to Jesus (see Revelation 5), but here the small letter "l" for lamb is used. Also never has Scripture described Jesus as a lamb with two horns or even one for that matter!

There is some interesting information on the horned kingdom in Revelation 17 that I would like to reveal. In verses 9 and 10, the seven heads are given two meanings. They are:

1. Seven mountains—"Seven heads are seven mountains, on which the woman sitteth" (verse 9), and verse 18 tells us "the woman… is that great city, which reigneth over the kings." What city is surrounded by seven mountains? Rome is, and it is indeed a great city. The Vatican City, a city in a city, is headquarters for the Roman Catholic Church. Are we finding reference to this re-ligion as the Mystery Babylon? Will the ten horns be headquar-tered in Rome, though separate from the church? Here is one more surprise—The ECM is indeed headquartered in Rome! Strange coincidences; strange, indeed! More to be said about this in another issue.

2. Seven kings—In verse 10, the seven heads are also described as "seven kings." This is reference to all the Gentile nations who have dominated Israel. It is building upon the symbolic "Man of Metals" in Daniel 2. Five were revealed from Daniel's time to the end times. Two nations ruled over Israel prior to this time. This is the breakdown:
   - Egypt—fallen
   - Assyria—fallen

- Babylon—fallen
- Media-Persia—fallen
- Greek Empire—fallen
- Roman Empire—currently is (at the time of this writing)
- Ten Horns—to come
- Beast and Ten Horns—last to come

This concludes this series on the Beast and the Ten Horns. As you can see, there is much that needs to be developed. So there does seem to be time yet, but it should be clear that the stage is indeed being prepared. There is simply too many potentials in this decade.

The very fact that a person such as myself has been given divine insights into this difficult subject is evidence of how close we are. The rapture, an event that could happen any day, has been a long anticipated occurrence. Unfortunately, few truly believe in the rapture, including most within the Christian faith. And it's this unbelief which will traumatize the saints who are left behind. The door will still be open, but many, if not all, will be tried and suffering will be the norm. Those who come through, whether by being a survivor after Armageddon or through a sacrificial death in the name of Jesus (Tribulation Saints), are who I think about most.

Let us not be like the Pharisees, all knowing in their religious pride. Their error should be our gain—consider it and be acceptable to the Lord. Whatever your doctrine or denomination, review it to be sure that it is the truth (biblically speaking). If you find it difficult to believe in the power of the Lord as demonstrated in the Bible, I can assure you the power will not be of much assistance in your hour of need. I feel it is the rapture itself which will aid tremendously in the acceleration of all seemingly impossible future events. Once you consider the rapture, all things become possible. I conclude with this one thought: "Faith is the substance of things hoped for, the evidence of things not seen" (Hebrews 11:1).

Gregory A. Booker

FOR THE RECORD—AS AN AFTERTHOUGHT on this day (23 July 1992), I request of my readers to consider the dates of when my letters were written. The first page of each letter has a date, and all letters took no more than three days to complete. The first letter took only two hours. Consider this information—The first letter was written before Operation Desert Storm (August 1990). The second and third letters prophesied a peace treaty to come, and such was not attempted until September 1991 between Israel and the Arabs. The USSR did not disband until January 1992, and weather catastrophes have intensified, creating burdens. May these insights further support my calling and your calling.

LETTER V

Dated 6 May 1991

Who is Mystery Babylon? John 21:15–25

JOHN 18 REVEALS PETER'S EARLIER denial of being with Christ during the trial, as Christ had prophesied Peter would do, not once but three times. And so it was. In John 21:15–17, Christ, after his resurrection, approaches Peter while they're fishing and asks Peter during mealtime, "Simon… lovest thou me?" three times, and Peter responds favorably three times. Christ then gives Peter direction to "feed my sheep" three times also.

Is Jesus clearing Peter's earlier denial by having him confess his love three times and subsequently provide instructions for Peter to feed his sheep without guilt? Peter did in fact preach the gospel as proven by the two books written by him—First and Second Peter. He was also considered the leader of the disciples.

In John 21:18–19, Jesus reveals information to Peter about Peter himself. Peter always did what Peter wanted to do; however, it is clear that he has decided to walk according to Christ. Christ knew he would. "But when thou shalt be old" (a prediction in itself) "thou shalt stretch forth thy hands." Could Jesus be revealing to Peter the timing of his death and also that his death will glorify God? Peter did, in fact, glorify God by requesting his crucifixion on the cross be upside down, for he was not worthy to die upright as Christ did. Peter's death occurred approximately forty years later. However, notice that Christ reveals to Peter something else in verse 18. After his death, "and another shall gird thee, and carry thee whither thou wouldest not." History has confirmed Peter's walk in Christ, and it must be recognized that Christ could be speaking prophetically, considering Peter's death did not occur until forty years later. Who is the "another" and why is Jesus revealing him to Peter?

In verses 20–21, Peter immediately recalls the situation at the Last Supper when John asks the question of who shall betray Jesus. (See John 13:21–30 for details.) However, this was related to Judas who had already hung himself. Peter shows to Jesus, without identifying John but by implicating him by "turning about" in John's direction, and asks Jesus, "What shall this man do?"

Could this be another example of Peter's impulsiveness thereby being confused and "thinks" of John as also betraying Jesus? I believe Peter is on the right subject (betrayal) but is thinking in the past about the wrong person (John). After all, Christ is speaking of the future and Christ Himself made no reference to John—that was Peter's mistake.

Jesus attempts to correct Peter's false assumption in verse 22: "If I will that he tarry till I come…follow me?" There is something being said here without saying it at all.

At this point, two facts are clear. First, our subject of concern is that betrayal will occur, and verse 18 also implies that it shall be as Peter would not have it. Second, history reveals that John never did betray Peter or Christ. He later wrote New Testament books, as well. Therefore, these facts should acknowledge that Peter's implication of John was in error. Jesus is not the author of confusion. However, could Peter be confused and it's Peter's assumption that Jesus is speaking of a man?

I believe that Christ is providing to future generations a betrayal to come in the name of Peter. The key is "till I come." This implies something unique, which the apostles alluded to in verse 23 when they said, "that that disciple should not die." Could our Lord be revealing a spiritual being who certainly can tarry till I come…if I will? All men must die; therefore, John could not possibly meet the condition "till I come." It's been almost two thousand years and counting. Could our Lord be warning us of a spiritual being to come in Peter's name and also is Christ exonerating Peter from any blame?

CONCLUSION

Again, can the future unlock the past? Who is "and another?" Time once again reveals the power of the Word of the Lord. The "Angel of Light," God's adversary—is he the "and another"? History confirms that the Roman Catholic Church is founded on the name of Peter. However, Peter would be more than happy to tell all that he is not the founder of the Roman Catholic Church. Even the history books reveal that it was the desire of the Roman Catholic Church to select Peter's name. The line of the apostolic fathers that Catholicism claim is not a biblically recognized doctrine.

I have reviewed other scriptural interpretation on this part of the Book of John and have found them wanting. The Jews were often confused by the revelations Jesus revealed to them. The Jews asked all the questions, exposing their ignorance, while we, the Gentiles, received the answers without such a "public risk." This is another example of the root. It does not surprise me that Peter was confused. There is a tremendous amount of prophetic undercurrents throughout the apostle's books. Would I have been any wiser in their time? I sincerely have my doubts.

MYSTERY BABYLON—A FALSE RELIGIOUS SYSTEM

REVELATIONS 17

Of all the chapters in the Book of Revelations, chapter 17 is the most heartbreaking to discuss. I do not desire its truths that our Lord reveals, but I do accept them nonetheless. It is sad that such deception can overcome so many people throughout the generations.

The Book of Revelations was written in approximately 95 AD. The error that both the Jew and Gentile made against the Sinless One, Christ, sealed the fate of man. First, the Jew endured the destruction of the Jewish Temple in 70 AD and their subsequent and eventual worldwide dispersion. Then the Gentile is evident in the Book of Revelations. There are unbelievers in both groups, if not in God, then in His Word!

Can we say that Christ, more so than any man who ever lived on this planet, was undeserving of such death, due to his sinless nature throughout his trials and crucifixion? And if there is one who must judge the sins of mankind, it is He and He alone who is worthy! God has shown us His righteousness and that He will not and cannot allow man in his sinful state a place in His kingdom. For if one is permitted, then all must be permitted, including God's real adversary—the first sinner who elected free will over God's will, none other than Satan. If Satan could not defeat Christ in the flesh, he has absolutely no hope on Judgment Day. The adversary now works through deception, constantly and without mercy. He is called, "appearing" as an Angel of Light. I have asked, Why is he allowed to be so effective in his works? The answer is again one of simplicity—Adam chose the same thing Satan did and that was the use of free will, also known as my will, and finally, I will.

It is now so clear that the best will is the will of the Creator. For it is His will which knows what is best for the creation. And the Bible clearly reveals His will while man desires free will. Can it be said that free will is the vehicle which permits sin to exist? Can one have free will and yet be sinless? Did not Christ Himself accomplish this feat like none other? God states, "We are all born sinners." Yes, we were all born with free will also. I believe the angelic realm has free will; however, the glory of God's power was so consuming that they elected, without question, God's will until a creation known as Lucifer spoke the words…"I will" (1 John 3:4–10 and Ezekiel 28:12–19). Man seems to have been created to allow the adversary an opportunity to present his case. And God, once again, makes the most out of the least. God makes it so clear that man, in his current state, has a beginning and an ending. Man, utilizing free will, seeks to contradict God's conclusions, and the adversary steps in to assist man's use of his free will by deception.

Mystery Babylon is the culmination of the most widespread deception since the ascension of Christ. It's beginnings are remarkably revealed in John 21:15–25. This passage is the last of the last gospel, the final words to Peter. Is it not John who wrote the Book of Revelations and added clarity to this "and another" perhaps clears himself? I am a firm believer that in some instances it requires the future to occur in order to know the past. Mystery Babylon is becoming less of a mystery and more of a fact. Let us measure the words of truth.

CAN MYSTERY BABYLON BE REVEALED?

An Overview of Christianity

Let's take a close look at what history has already provided us. This is my attempt to simply present, before all, basic doctrinal practices that existed long before our generation was ever thought of, and to provide a general understanding that while there are many doctrines, there is only one truth and only one source for the truth. Let it be known that the Bible supports doctrines, but it does not support doctrine which deviates from the Bible. The Bible represents God's perspective, and it is His perspective that I desire to reveal. May the Spirit of Truth be my guide in this challenging subject. Shall we begin?

From the time of the apostles until 300 AD, Christianity spread throughout the Roman Empire, in spite of frequent persecution. In 313 AD, Constantine the Great granted religious toleration to the Christians. This period was marked also by the definition of Christian dogmas and by recognition of the supremacy of the bishop of Rome. St. Linus is recorded as the first bishop of Rome after the death of Apostle Peter.

The growth of papal authority was gradual. After the destruction of Jerusalem in 70 AD, churches throughout the Roman Empire began to look to the church of Rome for leadership. Since the church was virtually the only civilizing and intellectual influence in the West during the

Middle Ages, it became customary to refer spiritual and moral and even political issues to the pope.

THE CATHOLIC BRANCH

Catholics believe their church is of divine origin. They believe Jesus Christ created His Church when he said to Peter, "Thou art Peter, and upon this rock I will build my church..." They also believe Christ guaranteed that Peter and his successors would be divinely preserved from error in preaching the truths entrusted to them. Thus, the pope can never be wrong when he speaks on faith and morality. The Catholics show special veneration for the Blessed Virgin Mary. They pray to her, and she intercedes with Christ for them.

Key Catholic Doctrine

1. The church is one in doctrine, authority, and worship.
2. The church is apostolic—descended in a direct line from the Apostle Peter—and is the only church from the time of the apostles.
3. It is catholic, or universal. Not only is it true to Christ's commission to teach all nations, but also it, and it alone, has the full body of truth taught by Christ.
4. The church is holy. It carries Christ's living message to the world. The church has a power that "helps" man to attain holiness.
5. The church ordains purgatory, a place or state of punishment wherein the souls of those who die in God's grace may make satisfaction for past sins and so become fit for heaven.

Points to Ponder

- While I believe the earliest intentions of the apostolic popes were to stay true to Peter's teachings, it is most clear that such a pure following did not continue.
- Notice also how their doctrine gives a "person" divine control, which also gives him "divine powers" over his subordinates.
- The longevity of the church is peculiar, especially when we consider in Daniel 2:40–43 the continued presence of the iron (Roman Empire) in the feet near the end times. If there is anything reminiscent of the old Roman Empire, is it not the city of Rome and its church, Roman Catholic?
- The glaring unbiblical doctrine of purgatory is in itself enough to reveal a false religious system. It is amazing that despite the

obvious error more than half of Christians are Roman Catholics.

- Could the deception be that while they accept Christ's divinity, they overrule the biblical writers by "adding doctrine." I ask all— who truly benefits by this tactic and where is the Bible?
- Notice also how the Catholics "share" the divinity of Christ by praying to Mary, confessing their sins and receiving forgiveness to and from a priest, and also acknowledging another man as "father." It is as if this is an attempt to replace God and the Son. I certainly do not see this as glorifying our Creator and His work!

THE PROTESTANT BRANCH...A RESPONSE

The term "Protestant" arose in Germany from the protest of the Reformation leaders against decisions of the Catholic majority around 1550 AD. The protest defended freedom of conscience and the rights of the minority. The Protestant Church became one of the three main divisions of Christianity, the others being the Roman Catholic and the Eastern Orthodox branch.

Key Protestant Doctrine

1. The Bible is the primary authority in matters of faith and practice. Conservative Protestants tend to interpret the Bible literally.
2. They believe in a "universal priesthood" of believers, in which all have access to God's grace without mediation of an ordained clergy. They also believe in salvation and justification by God's grace through faith alone. God's grace is not earned by good works as in Catholicism. And they believe man has free will to accept or reject grace.
3. They do not believe in an institution founded upon the divine authority of the clergy.
4. They also believe in the right for private judgment in religion.

Points to Ponder

- It appears that truth has a way of revealing itself after the deception is magnified. The Protestant Church came to be because of a rejection of what Catholicism was.
- Notice the emphasis on God's Word, the Bible, and God's grace.
- They recognize that Christ is a personal Savior to the individual and that salvation is not denominationally guaranteed.
- Let us be mindful that there are "problems" in this branch also. Many questionable doctrines have been so-called "inspired" that

are not of the writings of the apostles (The Bible). Be wary of them! The Bible is complete, and the primary source of inspiration is "divine interpretation" of God's Word. And the purity of the inspiration is founded solely on the ministry of Christ and Christ alone.

SCRIPTURAL ANALYSIS OF REVELATION 17

WHAT IS MYSTERY BABYLON GUILTY OF AND WHO ARE THE VICTIMS?

Verse 6 of Revelation 17 provides a most vivid answer. "She" was guilty of being drunken with the blood of the saints and the martyrs of Jesus. It is peculiar that two classes of the same kind of believers are being referred to. Why the separation? The saints are those who are martyred during the yet-to-come tribulation period. However, the martyrs of Jesus provides an interesting clue as to the longevity of the crime "she" is guilty of. "She" seems to only be guilty since the beginning of the time of Christ, particularly since the early development of the Christian church and throughout its history.

Literal Babylon has no impact here, and history reveals that the best way to challenge a religion is to do it with another religion. History also reveals the Roman Empire and its church, Roman Catholicism, have been guilty of martyrdoms throughout many centuries and many lands upon those desiring the true Christian doctrine as written.

In verse 1, Jesus calls Mystery Babylon a great whore. In verses 3, 4, and 6, John (the writer) simply calls her a woman. Why? The term "whore" is frequently used to symbolize a spiritual departure from God and His truths by an individual, city, or nation. The Lord knows this great departure from His truths is to come and forewarns all. But from John's perspective, he sees a woman, a beautifully adorned woman. He admires her, not recognizing her deception. John emphasizes appearance as acceptance! As is so much the case even today. Two different "views" are revealed by our Lord—His and man's. That is why in verse 7 the angel said, "Wherefore did thou marvel?"

In verses 2 and 4, "she" is guilty of another sin—her acts of fornication. Verse 5 identifies her as a Mother of Harlots. The term "harlots" refers to the many branches which have sprung from her and have been as apostate as her. Fornication indicates an act of spiritual deception applied to an individual before they are able to know the truth for themselves; thereby causing the "kings" to grow under her and to adhere to her, as so often has been the case. Once a Catholic, is he not always a Catholic simply by birth? Is he or she not tainted from the very beginning? A great way to assure membership, for the problem isn't getting in but it's how to get out!

THE ANGEL INTERPRETS

In verse 7, the angel makes clear to John that he will "tell the mystery of the woman." Let's see what kind of clues the angel gives about the woman. In verse 9, the angel tells us where the woman sits, or in other words, where her location is. She rides the ten-horned beast with its seven heads representing seven mountains. Does this mean she is located where she is surrounded by seven mountains? And here is wisdom—the city of Rome is indeed surrounded by seven mountains. Check your encyclopedias please! But is the woman a city?

In verse 18, the angel makes clear the woman is also representative of a city, a great city. Rome is not obscure but is indeed a great city! The ten kings shall also be in this city. To date, the European Common Market is indeed headquartered there, although the ten kings have not arrived in the final political structure.

I forewarn all that Rome is a respected power broker in the world today. Whether it supports political or religious issues, it's opinions are broadcasted and published throughout the world. Please exercise caution concerning their viewpoints. I do not suggest a blanket statement of disagreement against their policies. Simply weigh them in the balance in light of these alarming coincidences. Alarming, indeed!!

In verse 15, the whore has a following of many nations, people, tongues, and multitudes. And so the Roman Catholic Church does have such a diverse following…another coincidence. Verse 1 also states she sits upon "many waters."

In verses 16–17, judgment is passed, and the ten kings come against the religious system and destroys her. It is remarkable that the actual location is given. The challenge in these discoveries is to believe what is literally being alluded to. At the time of the writings, Rome probably did not warrant such a profound judgment. But God knows the power of His adversary, who is an Angel of Light, and man's unwillingness to consider His truths and His alone. And here is wisdom: Literal Babylon (a religion based on idol worship, sorceries, witchcraft, astrology, etc.)

predominated man's earlier beliefs. So after God made truth known through Christ, Mystery Babylon became the predominant tool used by the adversary. They both shall come to fruition again in these present times. I have seen evidence of Literal Babylon taking shape, and it is most peculiar to see published articles coming from Rome concerning the opinions of a spiritual leader of a group called Chaldeans Catholic Rite based in Babylon of Iraq.

Yes, Babylon the city is being rebuilt at this moment, a peculiar link and perhaps a deadly one. Be forewarned! The final hour of life as we know it could be making a desperate plea for survival by the unbelievers. We who believe in spite of the trials will see the glorious coming of Jesus. God has no desire to destroy that which He created, but the unbelievers deny Him. So what is He to do when the time comes for our Lord and Savior Jesus Christ to rule? The stage is indeed being prepared, and the adversary has nothing to lose for he has lost already. Therefore, be strengthened, desiring the truth even if it hurts. The truth will always save you from error. Be Forewarned!

TRUTH DEFINED AND REQUIRED

The Bible is…Truth Defined!

Jesus left eleven disciples to reveal His work of salvation to the world. Through divine inspiration issued by the Holy Spirit, seven of his disciples wrote twelve of the New Testament books. They are now better known as the Apostles to Jesus Christ.

The apostle Paul was commissioned separate from the disciples for the primary purpose of preaching to the Gentiles. Paul was an example of God taking the least likely person (as Saul of Tarsus he was a Pharisee who hated and persecuted the followers of Christ) and using him to glorify the power and mercy of our Lord. How could an individual be so against Christ, and after the encounter on the "road to Damascus," suddenly speak so eloquently for Him and writing more New Testament books than all the disciples combined?

I am convinced that only a direct command to fill Paul with the Holy Spirit could achieve such a dynamic and pure change. None of the writers had books to read, and we must remember most were fishermen. Their writings have withstood two thousand years of challenge, and yet the words stand as Christ revealed them. God is truly showing His power.

I say all this to drive home a point. There is indeed a purposeful containment of God's Word. The Book of Revelations, written by John, Christ's last living apostle, does a splendid job of concluding God's Word to man. Therefore, on what basis do we get so many "other views" that are clearly not according to the Bible? Is it intentional or preference or simply desired ignorance better known as free will?

Let us measure truth…case in point! There is a verse which gives much insight into what supports truth. Our court system is founded on this very principle. Mark 14:56 states, "For many bare false witness against him (Jesus), but their witness agreed not together." Much is said…let's examine!

If a victim is accused by his assailants and, under separate interrogation, their testimonies do not agree, they lose credibility and the victim's testimony is weighted as the truth. Now notice:

- Islam calls Jesus a prophet but not the Son of God.
- Jehovah's Witnesses call Jesus an archangel.
- Roman Catholics equate Mary Immaculate equivalent to Jesus (downgrade). Note: The Holy Spirit is our only intercessor!
- Mormons consider Jesus a son of God who did a great work but not The Son of God, Lord of Lord, and King of Kings.

Do you see that they bare false witness for they do not agree but choose to believe what they desire regardless of Christ's testimony? Therefore, do they not lose credibility and Christ, the victim, His words stand tall as the truth? However, in their attempt to be legitimate, there is one telling observation. They all use the Bible as a starting point, and *then* introduce their opinions as doctrine. Is it inspired or is it deception supported by preference (free will)? The adversary to God is indeed an Angel of Light. He establishes an apostolic line of fathers similar to the seed of David, demands that he be called "father," has doctrine that has no biblical support, and yet his church is accepted and respected worldwide—a deception that can only be defeated by truth!

It is important to focus on the obvious which can be surprisingly overlooked when "What is truth?" is the question. Let it be said that God Himself is the orchestrator of the Bible. Not one word is without His inspiration. All the writers of the New Testament were under the direct control of the Holy Spirit. You say, where's the proof?

The only writers of the New Testament were those who were direct witnesses of Jesus's divine nature. Paul was the exception; however, the use of someone such as Paul adds tremendous credibility to all the writers. For no man so far removed from the original disciples and Christ Himself could have harmonized his writings with the other New Testament writers without divine intervention. In other words, God has used eight witnesses and none…no, not one…disagree with the other!

Is truth defined or is it not?

IN CONCLUSION

As a final word of caution, when you examine the detailed information provided by Revelation 17 concerning Mystery Babylon, it is absolutely remarkable how clear the picture is made. The Roman Catholic Church with its erroneous doctrine was founded on deception in its beginning. God clearly has a day set aside for their fall. All I can say at this point is that man has free will and must elect to judge doctrine and, above all, desire it, if not insist on knowing the truth. That is perhaps the most important function of the Bible and the main provision of the Holy Spirit. But you must ask the question so He can give the answer!

God desires "the meek," not so much the weak. The weak stand to follow in any direction, calling themselves strong in their numbers but the meek will strive to use discretion. Character has a lot to do with how we walk. It is the Word of the Lord that the meek listens to. The world is measured against His Word. I forewarn all that doctrines do not always follow His Word. They may carry the Bible but do not fully examine it. They take out what they want, but not what they truly need to assure the salvation of the soul.

In closing, I want to clarify my intentions concerning the Roman Catholic Church. While it is a religious institution which deviates from the Bible, it is not the only one! Do not Islam, Hindu, Buddhism, and countless others qualify also as a false religious system? However, the Catholic Church is the world's largest, richest, and most influential religious presence acknowledged on earth. It is peculiar that the church prays to and through Mary, a woman of which Mystery Babylon is identified with. So many can be manipulated by "appearance." Let me say this, I am sure that there are members within the Catholic Church who seek Jesus and Jesus only and thus are saved. I pray this hope continuously! But let us remember that our Lord is a personal Savior, not a denominational one. Therefore, we are saved by faith and not by our works. Christ has performed the work and He Himself said in John 19:30, "It is finished." Repent and accept the handiwork of the Lord… Jesus is the perfect One!

NOTE: I write this letter with reluctance and with speculation, but nevertheless I am moved by the Spirit of Truth. I seek to forewarn! And personally, "I would rather be wrong and live this life in ridicule, than be right and live in heaven alone…knowing that I was afraid to tell you the truth." I have found His amazing grace. (John 16:13 and 2 Peter 1:18–21)

Gregory A. Booker

INSPIRED WRITINGS

THE PASTOR AND THE PROPHET

These are the words the Lord has spoken:

For our determination has been found before His throne

And He has heard the desires of our hearts.

And so a place shall be established…yea

A habitation that the Spirit of Him might dwell

In the fullness of His Truth.

And in My house shall tears be brought before My altar.

That there should be joy and joy unspeakable.

For who can know me lest my righteous judgment touch thee.

So let the minister lead and shall the prophet proclaim.

Let the minister protect and the prophet advise.

And shall my minister build the walls

But my prophet shall be without blueprint.

For he is mine!

Let these things be.

Lest the congregation be overwhelmed

And My Word becomes hindered.

Therefore, I sanction thee to work well in My House.

For the work of the ministry is for

The perfecting of the saints

That they might know the fullness of Him whom I have sent.

Therefore, bring me the fruit of their repentance.

That my Spirit might settle upon the weak,

And the lame, the hurt, and the fearful.

Yea, even the poor and the lost who need to be found.

I counsel thee to stand at the door of My gate and

Sound the trumpet of departure that they might taste

That which is hope and hear that which is pure.

Sound it well that my Spirit might hear thine expectation!

And know for a certainty thy precious faith.

That it is in my Son, the Christ, the Blessed Redeemer.

Hold fast to that which is true, my Church.

For the God of Israel is set to speak once again.

And it is His righteousness, which shall be declared by his prophets.

So gather the flock my ministers!

That we shall make way for the Lord of Lords and King of Kings,

Savior to the Gentiles and Messiah to the Jews. Amen!

To the Churches, let us place these words in the center of our hearts
that they might be found at the entrance of His Church.

LETTER VI

First Week of July 1991

Israel's Promised Redemption and the Tribulation Saints

The Choice: Truth or Religion

WHEN ALL IS SAID AND done, let it be said that my main theme throughout these "letters of prophetic utterances" is that the True God (He who demonstrates Himself) is not a religion. Man has always had a "religion" of some form or another. Before Jesus, man believed in idol worship and in many gods of which none were the same from culture to culture. The multiplicity of man-made gods is staggering when one looks at ancient history. From the hidden tribes of Africa to the Roman Empire, man attributes "someone else" for his being. God, in His infinite wisdom, used Israel to demonstrate Himself through. Let it be said that Israel failed God. But even this fact had to be proven, not to God Himself but to man. A personal Savior was promised from the Book of Genesis—before Israel existed. That Savior came, but was He not rejected?

The result of that rejection produced blessings for all men. Yes, the error of the Jews aided God in demonstrating His eternal existence to all men. The impact of Christ's resurrection changed the course of the world overnight. In principle, man went from believing in many gods to belief in one God. Idolatry was struck down conclusively. It is Jesus and Him alone who is responsible for such a phenomenon.

With truth revealed and idolatry recognized for what it was, a new form of "religion" erupted. The best word to describe this new approach is known as doctrine. Doctrine defined is "that which is taught and put forth as truth." Just like ancient man who had many gods. modern man has many doctrines. The guise of religious freedom is a deceptive one. Man is always accountable for his beliefs and confuses the right to accept or reject Christ as permission for electing other forms of religion. Man truly sinks his own ship, and this error hides the truth more than reveals it, does it not?

When Jesus walked among his own. it was the Pharisees who believed that their oral law (interpretations of law by rabbis, a religious traditions not recorded in the five books of Moses) was of equal importance with the inspired written law issued by God Himself. What actually blinded the Pharisees was their refusal in accepting the Word as the Word was given. Traditional practices crept in, and they fell prey to their own wisdom. For it is written in Proverbs 2:6, "The Lord giveth wisdom and out of His mouth cometh knowledge and understanding."

It is written in John 1:1, "In the beginning was the Word, and the Word was with God, and the Word was God," and verse 10 says, "He was in the world." He is the First Word and the Last Word! Let us remember that Jesus was prophesied to come and walk among men to fulfill the promises, thereby legitimizing his authenticity. He is better than religion ever could be, for He is the Only Truth.

More than three hundred prophetic Scriptures relate to Christ's first coming, and the Jews ignored every last one of them. I ask all "Why?" For the purposes of this letter, the Spirit sums it up in one word—tradition! Mark 7:8–9 and 13 says, "For laying aside the commandment of God, ye hold the tradition of men, as the washing of pots and cups... And he [Jesus] said unto them, Full well ye reject the commandment of God, that ye may keep your tradition...which ye have delivered: and many such like things do ye."

Tradition defined is "that which is transmitted orally through successive generations without the aid of written memorials." It is also any belief, custom, or way of life which has its roots in one's family or racial group. The most important part of the definition of tradition is that it is "oral transmission" by man, *not* a written revelation from God. This distinction is most critical for this is what separates truth versus religion and the Church of Christ from churches. Tradition is what blinds Christianity as God demonstrates the truth.

For the most part, we know what truth is, but I ask you this: Where is truth? This is the greater question in our generation. In other words, as Christians, should we be asking the question that tradition itself has caused us to be blinded to? It's a very basic question, but perhaps once asked, we could begin the process of removing the blinders. In the Bible, we do not find a nation called America, we do not find Asia, we do not find Africa or Europe or Russia—but we do indeed find Israel!!!

If "the Gentiles" never received the Bible, Christianity as well as Islam would never had been. Yet the Bible is written by the Jewish people by the authority of God Himself. All objective evidence and concepts would be unknown to men who sought spiritual discernment. It is alarming that just when Judaism is making a resurgence that elements of Christianity and Islam have the appearance of being "in agreement" regarding Israel. If we consider the restoration of Israel as God ordained (biblically stated), it stands to reason that all other prophetic acts should be realized in a literal sense also. Let it be said that the question is not "Whose side is God on?" Instead the question should be "Whose side are we really on?" Is it religion or is it truth, which is the ultimate redemption of Israel as the Bible proclaims it?

In other words, Christianity itself is so caught up in tradition (self-proclaimed doctrine) that truth is not being acknowledged when God Himself reveals it openly and plainly for all men. Yes, Israel is the truth and that is no religion. Indeed, I see the jealousy. I see the envy; their hearts are indeed prepared to boast!

I forewarn all—Never mind that the Jews may reinstate Judaism, never mind their unbelief in Jesus, never mind their zeal and pride or their lack of zeal for the Lord. The judgment is the Lord's! Woe, is there not also the unbelieving Gentiles who must be judged? As one who studies the prophetic Word of the Lord, I know certainly that such was prophesied to be. And so it is written:

"Boast not against the branches. But if thou boast, thou bearest not the root, but the root (Israel) thee…For I would not, brethren, that ye should not be ignorant of this mystery, lest ye should be wise in your own conceits; that blindness in part has happened to Israel, until the fullness of the Gentiles be come in. And so all Israel shall be saved: as it is written." (Romans 11:18, 25–26)

May those verses be wisdom.

Therefore, the error shall be made, for every man sees it right in his own eyes, but the Lord pondereth the heart. So I ask you another question: "What and who shall Israel be saved from?"

AND WHO SHALL BE THEIR SAVIOR? WHY I SEE WHAT I SEE!

AFTER MAKING NUMEROUS ATTEMPTS AT proclaiming the prophetic word to all kinds of people from various religious denominations, I began to understand why others do not see what I see. Some of the most staunch resistance has come from "church folks" who cannot seem to acknowledge the genuineness of prophecy. This lack of acknowledgment is primarily due to poor doctrinal insight and, yes, traditions! Jesus made it clear to "Watch therefore"! I advise everyone to read Matthews 24:42–51 and Matthews 25:1–13. Notice that Jesus is warning two different groups. In chapter 24, Jesus is speaking to the Jews about the Jews. In chapter 25, He is speaking prophetically about the churches. Verse 10 gives us a clear indication of a "sudden disappearance of believers in Christ." (See also 1 Thessalonians 5:9). Verse 22 reveals the agony of those left behind. These and others who become believers after witnessing what is known as "the rapture" are indeed the tribulation saints.

I see "these things" not so much because I study prophecy but because I believe Jesus is the Son of the Living God. As an agent of God Himself, His words will fulfill themselves to the very last letter. God is absolute; it is man who is relative. If one chooses to believe only so much of the Bible, then God is just in revealing only what you want to believe. I realize that prophecy has been a "mystery" to the church. However, the veil must be lifted. If God provided prophetic information to the Jews during Jesus's first appearance, do you think He would have the Church ignorant of his second coming? God is always fair. He does not change, but unfortunately, neither does man learn!

FOR CLARITY'S SAKE: WHAT IS A PROPHET?

- Prophets are those who speak for God. See Acts 3:21 and Hebrews 1:1.
- They are primarily preachers of righteousness. The most genuine prophets do not honor the pride of men. For they know the ways of the Lord in a most unique way due to an extreme submissive role. And they play no favorites. 1 Corinthians 14:3 reveals their purpose for the church.
- The spirits of the prophets are subject to the prophets. (See 1 Corinthians 14:29–33.) This means the church may have difficulty discerning what a prophet speaks since they know little about prophecy. However, this difficulty is somewhat diminished now that we have the written Word, the Bible, in our possession.
- We are told to covet prophecy. (See 1 Corinthians 14:39.)

The definition of "prophet" is "men divinely called and inspired to deliver God's message, particularly to future events." This definition matches the primary function of Old Testament prophets. In the New Testament, it refers to a person who has received a special spiritual gift, enabling him to interpret or proclaim truth. It does not necessarily involve the element of prediction. A prophet's key calling is "to reveal" or "to communicate or impart by supernatural means and to make known through divine inspiration something that was previously concealed."

Revealed theology means theology learned only by divine revelation.

I believe my writings reflect a "revealed theology" approach. For the events that I have come to know were through self-study and prayer and more prayer. The Holy Spirit does not require us to hold a degree in ministry; instead, we are to seek and to believe based on faith.

What makes a false prophet (self-proclaimed)?

1 John 4:1–3 tells the church to test the spirit of the prophet. The False Prophet will have a lack of confession publicly or in print that Jesus is God in the flesh. Anything else renders his message as not of the Holy Spirit. And only the Holy Spirit can reveal to us the truth as biblically stated.

A False Prophet Exemplified

More often than not, when the subject of prophets and their prophecies is brought into conversations, most "Christians" tend to listen to what the infamous French physician turned-prophet named Nostradamus has predicted. Due to his popularity, I think it best that I should highlight his "credentials" that we might better discern the spirit of a true prophet versus a false prophet:

The following is an excerpt from *A Critic's Analysis "Nostradamus and his Nonsense"* by James Randi: "The year 1999, seven months, from the sky will come a great King of Terror: To bring to life the great King of the Mongols, before and after Mars to reign by good luck."

Muddled or not, there it is: The fateful prediction from the most durable soothsayer of all times—the Renaissance prophet Nostradamus. To believers, it means the world will end in July 1999. Cagey and careful never to be too precise, Nostradamus divined the future events of the entire world before his death at age 63 in 1566. Like all physicians, he had cross-trained in astrology and eventually found it easier to prognosticate (do predictions). The critic discovered that Nostradamus often prophesied events that already occurred, blanketing them in murky symbolism. The seer skirted the Inquisition by attributing his prophecies to God and created many of the tricks still in use today by foretellers. Yet, close study finds his predictions, masked by smoke and mirrors, are open to any interpretation.

I classify Nostradamus as a false prophet, a soothsayer. Spiritually speaking, Nostradamus makes no proclamation of faith in Christ per 1

John 4:1–3. In my opinion, he is a tool of deception used by the deceiver. The biblical prophets are who I hear—Jeremiah, Isaiah, Daniel, Zechariah, Malachi, Joel, Paul, and Christ plus many others. May this insight add clarity and secure your faith in God Himself.

For the record, I classify myself as one "who works in the office of a prophet." This means that I do not emphasize calling myself a prophet but am called to speak on the subject that the biblical prophets speak of.

AFTER THE RAPTURE, A VEIL LIFTED

I HAVE SAID LITTLE CONCERNING the rapture—"for in a moment, in a twinkling of an eye…we which are alive and remain shall be caught up…to meet the Lord in the air" (See 1 Corinthians 15:50–58 and 1 Thessalonians 4:13–18). As one who believes that such an event will occur before the signing of the covenant with Israel, let it be known that this is one event that no man knows the day. However, I do recommend Hal Lindsey's book titled *The Rapture* which reveals much concerning this mystery doctrine, as the Scripture calls it.

My attempt at this point is to show the impact of such an event, regardless of when the event occurs. No greater event prior to the second coming will clearly and unquestionably demonstrate the presence of God Himself. I feel that this event is critical to giving hope to the tribulation saints. The saints represent anyone, regardless of their prior spiritual beliefs, who converts and accepts Jesus as the Son of God during the tribulation period.

Yes, a veil is indeed lifted. A mystery is no mystery any longer. The point is—could more people actually be saved by a pre-tribulation rapture than at any other time? In my opinion, yes! Does not the Book of Revelations become a spiritual guide which is much easier to understand for those who are living it? Does not the rapture shatter to pieces all tradition and false doctrine that has crept into Christianity? Indeed, it does! They will know their error and respond accordingly. The question will then be asked by the Lord. "As my Son has died for you, are you willing to die for Him?" What the saint really proves to God is that he believes Christ does indeed live. However, the sacrificial death represents their final testimony to that. It is the evidence of faith!

SCRIPTURE RELATED TO THE SAINTS

BOOK OF REVELATIONS: LETTERS TO THE CHURCHES

In principle, Jesus reveals the spiritual conditions of the various churches throughout the Church Age. Remnants of each abound today. Scholars have concluded the last church, Laodiceans, represent the spiritual state of Christianity in our generation. It is indeed so accurate (see 3:14–22). Let us strengthen ourselves so that we may indeed overcome.

6:9–11

The first heavenly cry of the saints is revealed. These are those who have been martyred after the rapture up to the opening of the fifth seal. This seal represents the mass persecutions against those who believe in God. Refusal to accept the mark of the Beast acts as way to conclusively separate the wheat from the tares. And so it is written that they are reserved for judgment. Jude 1:19 says, "These be they who separate themselves, sensual, having not the Spirit" or, in other words, those who buy the mark.

7:9–17

The separation is complete at the end of the great tribulation as verse 14 reveals. Verses 15–17 show their blessings being received. Notice who they serve—God Himself. But also notice who feeds them. Is it not the Lamb, Jesus? There is a distinction here. The great tribulation is identified as beginning in the middle of the Seventieth Week of Daniel and continues for the last three-and-a-half years of the "week." How can the rapture occur during the "week" and both groups have the same title of tribulation saints? They also appear to be more aligned with God, though blessed with Christ.

12:11

Reveals how the saints overcome the Antichrist by not accepting him even unto their death.

13:7–10, 14:11–13

Just what is the patience of the saints? The message here seems to be that he who resists the Antichrist with the sword shall die by the sword. He delivers his soul to hell since he did not willingly accept the condition of a sacrificial death in the name of Jesus. He therefore did not truly overcome. Is this not indeed faith and patience? Did not Christ willingly die for us?

20:4

"And I saw the souls of them that were beheaded for the witness of Jesus." As gruesome as this method may seem, this is what it accomplishes—there is no doubt in my mind that the Antichrist will generate more fear on modern society by using such an archaic method of persecution. But one advantage from the Lord's point of view is it is done in a twinkling of an eye and therefore it is painless. It's the thought that hurts. Look up and believe now, so that you may be where he is!

And may this be wisdom.

These things must be for the perfecting of the saints and to condemn those in their unbelief that they may be reserved for that great day of judgment in the Valley of Jehoshaphat where they go to destroy Israel, the only nation on earth that shall call for a Savior!

Thus Israel's promised redemption happens at last.

"For the Israelites will live many days without king or prince, without sacrifice or sacred stones, without ephod or idol. Afterward the Israelites will return and seek the Lord their God and David their king. They will come trembling to the Lord and to his blessings in the last days" Hosea 3:4–5 (NIV).

Scripture declares in Hosea 14:9, "Who is wise? Let them realize these things. Who is discerning? Let them understand. The ways of the Lord are right; the righteous walk in them, but the rebellious stumble in them."

ROMANS 11:26

"And so all Israel shall be saved: as it is written…"

(And where is it written? It is written in the Old Testament.)

And here is wisdom: As one man, Jesus, tested the nation of Israel, so shall such nation test the world. For it is not so much who is right, but who is the least wrong! His grace abounds. Prepare ye the way!

There is a rule in prophetic analysis that goes like this: If what you read in the Scriptures has not happened yet, that doesn't mean it won't!

THE CALLING!

Let us listen to the voice of the Lord speak to Israel in Ezekiel 34—

"As a shepherd seeketh out his flock in the day that he is among his sheep that are scattered; so will I seek out my sheep, and will deliver them out of all places where they have been scattered in the cloudy and dark day" (verse 12).

"Therefore will I save my flock, and they shall no more be a prey; and I will judge between cattle and cattle. And I will set up one shepherd over them" (verses 22–23).

"And they were scattered, because there is no shepherd: and they became meat to all the beasts of the field, when they were scattered... yea, my flock was scattered upon all the face of the earth, and none did search or seek after them" (verses 5–6). Never in the past have they been upon "all the earth," but they are now!

Joel 1:14

"Sanctify ye a fast, call a solemn assembly, gather the elders and all the inhabitants of the land into the house of the Lord your God, and cry unto the Lord."

Joel 2:17–18

"Let the priests, the ministers of the Lord, weep between the porch and the altar, and let them say, Spare thy people, O Lord, and give not thine heritage to reproach, that the heathen should rule over them: wherefore should they say among the people, Where is their God? Then will the Lord be jealous for his land, and pity his people."

Micah 4:6–7

"In that day, saith the Lord, will I assemble her that halteth, and I will gather her that is driven out, and her that I have afflicted. And I will make her that halteth a remnant, and her that was cast far off a strong nation."

Micah 5:7–8

"And the remnant of Jacob shall be in the midst of many people as a dew from the Lord, as the showers upon the grass...And the remnant of Jacob shall be among the Gentiles in the midst."

Micah 7:16

"The nations shall see and be confounded at all their might: they shall lay their hand upon their mouth, their ears shall be deaf."

Isaiah 11:10–12 (NIV)

"In that day the Root of Jesse will stand as a banner for the peoples; the nations will rally to him, and his resting place will be glorious. In that day the Lord will reach out his hand a second time to reclaim the surviving remnant of his people from Assyria, from Lower Egypt, from Upper Egypt, Egypt, from Cush, from Elam, from Babylonia, from Hamath and from the islands of the Mediterranean. He will raise a banner for the nations and gather the exiles of Israel; he will assemble the scattered people of Judah from the four quarters of the earth."

An example of Israel's error against Jesus and their subsequent dispersal and yet an eventual return:

Micah 5:1–3

"Now gather thyself in troops, O daughter of troops: he hath laid siege against us: they shall smite the judge of Israel with a rod upon the cheek. But thou, Bethlehem Ephratah [referring to Jesus who later was indeed born in Bethlehem and Israel did smite him], though thou be little among the thousands of Judah [Jesus's genealogy is from the tribe of Judah], yet out of thee shall he come forth unto me that is to be ruler in Israel; whose going forth have been from of old, from everlasting. Therefore will he give them up [were they not dispersed], until the time that she which travaileth hath brought forth: then the remnant of his brethren shall return unto the children of Israel [restoration]."

Analysis

Let us realize that the prophet Micah wrote these words in approximately 720 BC. His words are an example of the vastness of time it can take for certain events to be fulfilled. And notice how the certainty of events generates a reaction, for every bit of it was prophetic and all has occurred right on up to our time. The amount of time used to fulfill the events is beyond human control, yet man uses his free will in making the events come true. Clearly, this reveals that when man uses his own knowledge, ignoring the very words God forewarned him about, he fails God. God Himself is cleared of setting man up as a result. Numerous prophetic Scriptures reveal this "all knowing" phenomenon.

In essence, God is showing man with uncanny subtleness that God's will is supremely superior to the use of free will and most certainly the "I will." His love is demonstrated despite our errors. Israel has been his tool for just this purpose. At the appointed time, I personally want to stand before Him and glory in His presence. This I do pray! I now know why we need Jesus, yes, indeed!

JESUS FOREWARNS THE JEWS OF ANTI-SEMITISM

"AND YE SHALL HEAR OF wars and rumors of wars: see that ye be not troubled: for all these things must come to pass, but the end is not yet. For nation shall rise against nation, and kingdom against kingdom: and there shall be famines, and pestilences, and earthquakes, in divers places. All these are the beginning of sorrows. Then shall they deliver you [Jews] up to be afflicted, and shall kill you: and ye shall be hated of all nations for my name's sake" (Matthew 24:6–9).

God's mission to restore Israel will cause world strife.

"Behold, I will make Jerusalem a cup of trembling unto all the people round about, when they shall be in the siege both against Judah [interchangeable with Israel] and against Jerusalem. And in that day will I make Jerusalem a burdensome stone for all the people" (Zechariah 12:2–3).

A PURPOSE FOR WHICH GOD SHALL USE ISRAEL FOR…REVEALED!

"Then shall ye return [Israel], and discern between the righteous and the wicked, between him that serveth God and him that serveth him not" (Malachi 3:18).

Yes, I have searched for His wisdom, and He has given it. I could go on and on revealing these types of unusual writings. Some think that the Old Testament is a closed book. Let it be said that the restoration of Israel has opened it up. Yes, the true colors of an individual can be exposed, not so much by who they are with, but who they may be against! This is the heart of my forewarning.

JUDGMENT ASSURED

"AND AT THAT TIME SHALL Michael stand up, the great [angelic] prince which standeth for the children of thy people: and there shall be a time of trouble, such as never was since there was a nation even to that same time: and at that time thy people shall be delivered" (Daniel 12:1).

"Now also many nations are gathered against thee, that say, Let her [Israel] be defiled, and let our eye look upon Zion. But they know not the thoughts of the Lord, neither understand they his counsel: for he shall gather them as sheaves into the floor" (Micah 4:11–12).

"Therefore wait ye upon me, saith the Lord, until the day that I rise up to the prey: for my determination is to gather the nations, that I may assemble the kingdoms, to pour upon them mine indignation, even all my fierce anger: for all the earth shall be devoured with the fire of my jealousy" (Zephaniah 3:8).

"And it shall come to pass, that as ye were a curse among the heathen, O house of Judah, and house of Israel; so will I save you, and ye shall be a blessing: fear not" (Zechariah 8:13, see also chapters 12–14).

"And thou shalt come up against my people of Israel, as a cloud to cover the land: it shall be in the latter days, and I will bring thee against my land, that the heathen may know me, when I shall be sanctified in thee, O Gog, before their eyes" (Ezekiel 38:16).

The Book of Daniel identifies the conquest of the Antichrist as he gains power. However, the Book of Ezekiel reveals the battle of Armageddon (Chapter 38 and 39). Could Gog be his new designation after attaining world dominance; even the land of the uttermost north which scholars conclude is the now disbanded USSR? Could Gog be the Antichrist at the peak of his satanic rule over Earth? (God changed names and used additional names to identify and further clarify biblical characters many times in Scripture.) And Ezekiel 39:2 reads, "And I will turn thee back, and leave but the sixth part of thee, and will cause thee to come up from the north parts, and will bring thee upon the mountains of Israel."

In the New Testament, Jesus answers the Jews' question of when in Luke 21:25–58, "And there shall be signs in the sun, and in the moon, and in the stars; and upon the earth distress of nations, with perplexity; the sea and the waves roaring; Men's hearts failing them for fear, and for looking after those things which are coming on the earth: for the powers of heaven shall be shaken. And then shall they see the Son of man coming in a cloud with power and great glory. And when these things come to pass, then look up, and lift up your heads; for your [Israel's] redemption draweth nigh."

This is the great mystery revealed—Our Lord is Savior to the Gentiles, but can He not also be realized as the Messiah to the Jews at last?

THE BATTLE LOCATION

"I WILL GATHER ALL NATIONS, and will bring them down into the Valley of Jehoshaphat, and will plead with them there for my people and for my heritage Israel, whom they have scattered among the nations, and parted the land...Proclaim ye this among the Gentiles; Prepare war, wake up the mighty men, let all the men of war draw near; let them come up...Multitudes, multitudes in the valley of decision: for the day of the Lord is near in the valley of decision" (Joel 3:2, 9, and 14).

The element of surprise is ever present as He states so emphatically—"And they shall know that it is I, the Lord...who have spoken it!"

Oh, perhaps, our nuclear arsenal that we are so proud of will someday make the grace of God of none effect and God will have no choice but to make Himself known to the unbeliever. It is quite clear that His Word is written, despite our unbelief, and His foreknowledge is evident that we might know that there is a God and a merciful one indeed. Be forewarned!

IN CONCLUSION—STRANGE COINCIDENCES

I HAVE REVEALED ONLY A sampling of Scriptures related to an event that has never occurred in Israel's history. But the appearing of Jesus as Messiah is beyond human comprehension. How can man demand a person be sinless when he himself is not? How can words of the Scriptures cross time and, though written by men, be from the knowledge of men? I find even the term "many nations" peculiar in itself. No time in the past best meets that criteria except the present. With the exception of the Exodus, Israel has never been truly saved by such a glorifying event.

Another coincidence is that for the first time in man's development, he holds his own destiny. He has never been able to destroy himself, but with the advent of nuclear weapons, he can now. Our environment is being fractured without the use of such weapons already.

Be forewarned! God is indeed holding back man from destruction. As long as there are those who continue to proclaim the name of Jesus, God will postpone his wrath. The subject of God is in the news constantly, but I do notice a vacuum concerning His work—Jesus. It is a subtle absence, an eerie blank. For it is written in 1 John 5:10, "He that believeth on the Son of God hath the witness in himself: he that believeth not God hath made him a liar; because he believeth not the record that God gave of his Son."

The rapture ends God's restraint, then all must be fulfilled. A veil shall be lifted when the rapture proclaims itself to be what it must be, an ending and a beginning all wrapped up into one act. The tribulation saints are those who come to know the truth (that they refused to accept) as a result of the redemption of Israel. And so they shall be saved, as it is written. Stand back and pray. "Thou wilt perform the truth to Jacob, and the mercy to Abraham, which thou hast sworn unto our fathers from the days of old" (Micah 7:20).

And here is wisdom: In the name of religion, many will be more against God than for Him. For the truth is Israel, and God Himself shall proclaim it so. We are so close. Therefore, do not yield to the delusion that is to come. For its purpose is to align all unbelievers that they may be judged due to their unbelief concerning Israel. So shall the truth of Jacob be performed as promised as it is written. As the Jew, so is the Gentile! Thus, it is written, "And so all Israel shall be saved: as it is written, There shall come out of Zion the Deliverer, and shall turn away ungodliness from Jacob" (Romans 11:26). What should be obvious, obviously is not!

In closing, it is indeed a mystery when the very evidence (Israel's restoration) that there is a God is resisted and even despised by those who profess a belief in God—a mystery indeed. The Adversarial One, an angel "appearing as a light," the accuser of the brethren who walketh to and fro, yea up and down upon all the earth, a deceiver of men, and yes, some men prefer his way by their election of free will. I am indeed blessed to see an ending to these things and a beginning of a new and eternal blessing. Let the Bible be our anchor in the midst of the storm, for a storm there must be to try our faith and be found worthy and blameless so that we may partake of the glory that most assuredly must come. When all is said and done, I can only save myself. Therefore, by the reading of my words and the preaching of the gospel, may you elect to do the same for yourself. For the Prince of Peace cometh to put down all rebellion in those men who so desire it. Accept Him as your personal Savior and receive of the promises foretold. I have heard and do submit. Amen!

Gregory A. Booker

INSPIRED WRITINGS

THE OTHER SIDE OF THE CROSS
A Poem of Poetic Justice

There's something amiss when the creation resists all that the Creator
stands for.

As I gaze at the cross, it reflects a world lost

With Christ knocking on every door.

Man thinking himself good, did that which he thought he should,

With charges of blasphemy and plenty of religiosity,

Refused to believe the Word… being filled with animosity

Delivering the Lord to the court of courts.

And so the trial did promptly begin.

He was alone, having not a character witness, nor even a friend

And when the judge could find no law against him,

Washing his hands, I'm sure he did what he can.

All except free this sinless man.

"Crucify…crucify" was the outcry from the crowd!

And the Law that was became no Law at all, and yet God smiled!

So there our Savior laid with outstretched arms,

Demonstrating His love despite the harm.

And while every man is born in sin,

The injustice we profess doesn't compare to the injustice
He was placed in.

There's something amiss when the creation resists

All that the Creator stands for even now like then.

But an empty Tomb was God's reward for a work well done.

Not to be hid, the Lord shone forth His only Son.

For Jesus showed His love toward all mankind.

And now there is life after death in only His name you will find!

But let the Other Side of the Cross speak also.

That what and who we are has surely been exposed.

For in God's love so openly displayed,

We did show our wretchedness that day.

And God's Law of Love soundly defeated

Our law of justice, which we misdeeded.

Our anger truly showed only to see the peace of God flow.

Our fearfulness for no reason illuminated God's love for all seasons.

The Cross is the meeting place for all of this.

And believe it or not, the Creator let the creation insist!

So let us remember the wisdom the Cross is meant to bring.

God will have His day of justice that righteousness,
which is fairness, ought ring.

For the other side of the cross speaks well of His return.

Sitting on the right-hand side of the Father, this He earned!

But there are yet those who choose not to believe

Like doubting Thomas, they say "Not by faith but by sight must I see!"

But blessed are those who believe and have not seen!

For no more is God a mystery, neither is He a dream.

You see, grace and mercy have been born out of injustice.

And it is the other side of the cross that gives us this message.

That our way of justice means nothing
when truth demands His return.

For this is why the Word declares the Earth shall burn

And we who are caught up in His rapture shall bear witness.

Revealing that the Other Side of the Cross was
a lesson that went unlearned!

LETTER VII

Second Week of July 1991

The Christ and His Glorious Appearance

AND SO IT IS WRITTEN, "And I will put enmity between thee [the seed of the serpent which symbolizes the deceiver who used the serpent] and the woman, and between thy seed and her seed; it shall bruise thy head, and thou shalt bruise his heel" (Genesis 3:14–15). Genealogy requires all children to follow the seed of man but the Lord's reference to the seed of woman implies that such an enmity shall not be brought about by a child fathered by men.

And so it was a divine birth, a virgin birth, the only such birth. Is it not written in Luke 1:35, "The Holy Ghost shall come upon thee, and the power of the Highest…shall be called the Son of God"? And was not the enmity established as it is written in Matthew 2:13, "For [King] Herod will seek the young child to destroy him"? Herod was so desperate that he slew all children less than two years old in Bethlehem. It is unbelievable that an old king could be so threatened by a newborn child. I have learned from the Spirit of Truth that it was not so much the heart of man but the direct hand of the adversary seeking to invalidate the mission of God in providing a Savior for man. And Jesus had his "heel bruised." He was struck down, but His resurrection makes it very clear that He did not stay down!

Though the event was not recorded until the time of Moses, the words "heel bruised" were spoken at the time of the fall of Adam in the garden. Scholars date the time of Adam at approximately 4004 BC by using genealogical references given in the Bible. Yes, the Bible does a superior job of dating itself. Considering this, therefore, it took 4,000 years for the seed of woman to come and then have his "heel bruised." That is truly incomprehensible by the human mind, but did it not occur as it was written nevertheless?

Genesis 3:15 is the first reference to a savior in the Bible. It is also the oldest unfulfilled Scripture, for the fulfillment of "and it shall bruise thy head" has yet to be accomplished. The Bible makes it clear just how that will be performed. A 2,000-year wait for Christ's return can be understood when one considers the eternal nature of God.

At times I recognize the grace of God as simply one phenomenon, and that phenomenon is time. A good friend of mine defined time as distance. I do see his point, for without movement, time becomes irrelevant. Measuring distance qualifies time and gives it substance. Few people consider the impact of time (dates) when they study the Bible.

Time is the very thing which differentiates us from God. He is eternal; we are not.

Sin is the cause of such separation brought about by the offense of Adam. This separation is much better known as death, both in the flesh and in the spirit. Yes, even the spirit is separated from God *if* certain conditions are not met in this life, for hell is where heaven is not. God foreknew that man would need a savior greater than man himself for those who would desire to see the God that is. Let it be said that God is not going to lower His standards for us. It is far better for us to be elevated to His ideals, and I cannot blame Him one bit.

Yes, Israel failed thinking obeisance of the Law was enough. For man, maybe it was, but for God, it was not. God's criteria is higher. It is more than obeisance of the Law. It is also a heart without sin. Man never could accomplish that feat. So God birthed Himself among men to demonstrate a sinless way. And we all know what the law of man did to the Sinless One. Christ was entitled to strike back, but He did not, lest He sin and invalidate the very purpose for which He came.

And so it is written in Romans 5:18–19, "Therefore as by the offense of one judgment came upon all men to condemnation; even so by the righteousness of one the free gift came upon all men unto justification of life. For as by one man's disobedience many were made sinners, so by the obedience of one shall many be made righteous." Man indeed showed to himself the true nature of his character. Innocent men have been put to death before, but one without sin presents a greater injustice.

God states "He foreknew" the errors the Jews would make. Then why did He continue with it? He continued for the pure love of His creation—mankind. However, no matter how much love God had for us, His righteousness could not be lowered to compensate for man's error of sin, which is disobedience. The necessity of a substitute who would not sin in order to save himself became reality. Jesus paid that price, and the only reason he succeeded was because he was of God Himself. All his miracles were performed to reveal to us the kingdom of God and, in the process, defeat the adversary. Remember, we would not even know that there was an adversary without the sinless offering of Christ revealing him.

A sinless man found guilty with the Law ending in failure. And now the Messiah is justified, as witnessed by His resurrection, at the appointed time to make amends. In all honesty, don't you think He is entitled to judge? It saddens me how we hear mankind call out for justice when he has been treated unfairly, yet as Christians we hear not the call of the Lord for His Son to fulfill the "bruising of thy head." Yes, it was a mortal wound to Satan so that man may finally live the peace God so desired of him from the beginning.

DO WE NOT KNOW HIS RIGHT TO JUDGE?

FOR IS IT NOT WRITTEN, "In that day when God shall judge the secrets of men by Jesus Christ according to my gospel" (Romans 2:16).

God accomplishes much through Jesus—

- He reveals man's inability to measure righteousness using the Law.
- He reveals the nature of Himself.
- He sacrifices Himself for sinners.
- In spite of man's error against Him, He offers salvation to one and to all for their belief in Him as the Son of God.
- He reveals to man his character fault—sin.
- He defeats His adversary by refusing to sin unto death. Satan's error in the heavens was pride, which is a sin. Christ dying sinless in the flesh was the key to Satan's defeat. If Satan could not defeat Christ on earth, he is doomed in the heavens. He will be allowed to fight, symbolizing earth's struggle at the time of Christ's return, but his fate is determined.
- He establishes for Earth a new ruler, the Prince of Peace—Jesus!
- He permits man to condemn himself in his unbelief, and when the time for judgment has come, man will know his error.
- He demonstrates the power of love and faith and solidifies to man what truth is.
- He reveals victory over death through the resurrection.

God uses the very least possible—one man—to accomplish an endless message to man concerning His divine purpose. I now know the hidden meaning in the mustard seed parable used to describe the kingdom of God. Man has his hope planted in one seed, in one resurrection, in one act of salvation (See Mark 4:30–32). The second coming of

Christ is the sprouting of that seed in full bloom, overcoming all things on the earth so that all things will be better, better indeed!

PURPOSE OF THE SEVENTIETH WEEK OF DANIEL

AFTER KNOWING WHAT WILL HAPPEN, I am sure the question of why must it happen enters our mind. I have discovered that, when I accept God's perspective concerning what will happen, I am instinctually led to ask Him "why" and He provides the heavenly answer to earthly problems. I ask Him why an Antichrist, why the tribulation saints, why only one-third of Israel is saved during the final "week," and why death is so prevalent throughout the seven-year period. It is searching Him out daily and with much prayer that I have received divine insight into these sensitive and yet provoking questions.

The question of "why" is what the Holy Spirit is always prepared to answer. He tells me how "the why of it" indicates the answer will be heard and acknowledged by the receiver. He speaks according to our desire to know. My favorite Scripture that has guided me along this path is found in John 16:13—"Howbeit when he, the Spirit of Truth, is come, he will guide you into all truth: for he shall not speak of himself; but whatsoever he shall hear, that shall he speak: and he will shew you things to come."

In essence, if you fear the question, you stand never to receive the answer and the answer is only as good as the question you ask. Everything I received, I did indeed ask for. The answers I received concerning some of the most perplexing paradoxes in His prophetic word can be difficult to discern. If it is for me, I know it is for many of my readers as well. Therefore, let me reveal just a sampling of some "why's." And may it culminate in the second coming of our Lord and Savior for both the Jew and the Gentile who believes in His name.

PEACE AND SAFETY A PARADOX

IT IS WRITTEN IN 1 Thessalonians 5:1–3, "But of the time and seasons, ye have no need that I write unto you. For yourselves know perfectly that the day of the Lord so cometh as a thief in the night. For when they shall say, Peace and safety; then sudden destruction cometh upon them… and they shall not escape."

When we look at current world distress, most people conclude that the conflict between Israel and the Arabs is the most potentially dangerous conflict. Many feel it could actually ignite into a World War. As a result, it is always a politically delicate subject. The Middle East has many paradoxical situations, and if one tries to determine why based on what I call "the human realm," the answer can and will be quite different than in the "spiritual realm."

I no longer ask why these two nations are at each other's throats, but instead I ask what does God accomplish despite their hatred? My third letter, "The Paradox of the Seventieth Week," explains in detail this very phenomenon.

The day of the Lord appears to be parallel to when they say peace and safety. Then there is sudden destruction. What would make the world say peace and safety unless there was a real potential threat? And why does the achievement of it render God's wrath? The Spirit reveals that the answer is based on the conditions by which the peace is agreed upon. In essence, for a peace treaty to be signed, concessions will have to be made. These concessions will indeed have something to say about man's belief in God and the Bible.

The majority of Jews in Israel are still in unbelief about Jesus and even God Himself. And are not the majority of Gentiles in the world also in unbelief concerning God and His Son? Therefore, when the issue of peace is discussed, we must be acutely aware of not "who" is doing the negotiating but "what" is being negotiated. It is almost as if peace can never be reached as long as Israel is considered as the Promised Land. This is a subtle statement but a very powerful one indeed. Unbelievers seem to be caught in a vise on all sides. And they are! The Arabs and the Jews appear to use a god to justify their own purpose, a common practice among us all. It is written that Israel will put their trust in man once again. A signed peace treaty reflects their unbelief not only in Jesus (nationally, this is their stance currently), but also in God. Remember, there is always the remnant in Israel that will be saved when their eyes are opened.

Therefore, Israel will be represented by the False Prophet. He will seem to be the Messiah the Jews have been waiting for all along. It is written that "he" shall make a covenant with Israel. This "he" is the Antichrist, and he will represent the Arab's interest. I believe he will be an Arab. For the record, let's just say he will be like none other the world has ever known. His greatest achievement, when he comes, will be the success of a formal peace agreement with Israel.

The momentum is building up already. I believe many leaders throughout the world will offer their solutions but all will come up short until he arrives. He will be bold enough to discredit Christ publicly and receive worldwide support. Be forewarned, that it is the terms of the conditions that initiate the day of the Lord. The individual who solicits such terms will quickly become obvious to the churches. Many leaders around the globe acknowledge their religious beliefs, but few, if any, will publicly deny the deity of Christ—and that's the difference!

THE ABOMINATION OF DESOLATION

JESUS SPOKE IN MATTHEWS 24:15, saying "When ye therefore shall see the abomination of desolation, spoken of by Daniel the prophet, stand in the holy place, (whoso readeth, let him understand)." Daniel 9:27 reads, "…and in the midst of the week he shall cause the sacrifice… to cease, and for the overspreading of abominations he shall make it desolate." This will occur in the middle of the seven-year period. The last three-and-a-half years of this period are called the great tribulation. Jesus reveals this designation himself in Matthews 24:21. The abomination is described in 2 Thessalonians 2:4—"Who opposeth and exalteth himself above all that is called God, or that is worshipped; so that he as God sitteth in the temple of God, shewing himself that he is God."

In the Book of Revelation 13:5 it is written, "…and power was given unto him [Antichrist] to continue forty and two months." Clearly this is the beginning of the second half of the seven-year period, and he has even more power. His spiritual deception described in the above Thessalonians verse is further supported by his physical act described in Revelation 13:15 where it is written "And he had power to give life unto the image of the beast, that the image of the beast should both speak, and cause that as many as would not worship the image of the beast should be killed." This is the abomination of desolation spoken of. It is an act of desecration!

It is clear that the Jewish temple must be rebuilt to fulfill this act. To date, no such temple stands. But it is possible that, as a condition of peace, the Jews are allowed to build one without interference from the Arabs who despise such a project. I have a feeling that the issue of rebuilding the temple will create worldwide "interest and tension." It's amazing how certain unbelievers so vehemently reject incidents that are actually fulfilling biblical prophecy. It is almost as if they know but are intent on preventing it regardless of what God has revealed. The satanic forces are indeed quite aware and do they not show themselves and their work. But God will prevail, so I forewarn!

PURPOSE OF THE ANTICHRIST

God makes it clear that Satan is the ruler of this world but only for a time—thanks to Jesus. Through our free will, we elect to accept Christ; however, the Bible makes it clear that we are accountable for our rejection of Him as well. It is written in 2 Thessalonians 2:9–12, "Even him, whose coming is after the working of Satan with all power and signs and lying wonders, And with all deceivableness of unrighteousness in them that perish; because they received not the love of the truth, that they might be saved. And for this cause God shall send them strong delusion, that they should believe a lie: That they all might be damned who believe not the truth, but had pleasure in unrighteousness." I have no idea what this "strong delusion" could be, but I do believe that it will be so obvious as not being of God that the wicked will love it. It is no doubt in my mind that the Antichrist will lead them to accept it. Those who refuse to believe such a delusion as valid will be exposed and our faith will be tried.

The mark of the Antichrist separates the field and prepares the harvest for reaping. The Book of Revelations speaks painfully clear to those who accept the mark (see Revelation 14:9–20). God is allowing us through the use of our free will to elect our choice. It should become clear that God actually restrains Satan in all that he is allowed to do so that things may be achieved for a greater purpose. When all is said and done, God did not have to reveal these things. Let it be said that it is always better to know than to be ignorant for His instruction has indeed strengthened me and may it do the same for you!

THE BEGINNING OF THE END

IN THE FINAL ANALYSIS, WHEN I consider the magnitude of such an awesome conclusion to man, I cry. There are approximately five billion people on this glorious planet. They are of every shape, size, color, and temperament in every part of the globe, and all are from the seed of Adam. It is the varieties of men that has made life challenging yet heartbreaking. We all want a leader who can heal us of our wounds, provide us our needs, and perform justice when required. There is a civil order among men no matter who they are or where they may be. They must have a king, a president, a ruler, a leader. Even if he favors them not, man must have someone.

With all the races, ethnics, cultures, and political and religious differences, it will be quite a feat to make all men see eye to eye in principle. But this is exactly what the Antichrist will be able to perform. There will be few, if any, barriers among men as the Beast demonstrates himself. Simply put, all unbelievers with their many differing beliefs will be made to believe in one. For the real enemy in their hearts is the truth, which is the Christ. The many turmoils, from civil unrest to weather catastrophes, are placing a heavy burden upon our leaders throughout the world. As world distress increases day by day, men will come together in a New World Order, seeking a solution to appease everyone. Their ideals will be sweeter than mom's apple pie, but not even mom can make a good apple pie with rotten fruit!

Therefore, the Lord will let them have their day, and in their unbelief, He shall give them a leader, a leader they want so they can continue in their sins. Opportunity will be lost to them as they condemn themselves. He shall lead the Ten-Horned Kingdom, also known as the Ten Nations and classified as Ten Toes in the Book of Daniel. Daniel 2:40–43 identifies their mix as part iron and part clay. We know that Syria shall settle with Israel and the Antichrist shall be its leader. Four of the horns are revealed with the other three being Egypt, Greece, and Turkey. Therefore, can we say that the Ten-Horned Kingdom will be a European and Arab Alliance? Strange bedfellows, indeed, as iron is to clay!

And thus it is written in Revelation 13:5–8 (NIV), "The beast [Antichrist] was given a mouth to utter proud words and blasphemies and to exercise his authority for forty-two months. It opened its mouth to blaspheme God, and to slander his name and his dwelling place and those who live in heaven. It was given power to wage war against God's holy people [the saints] and to conquer them. And it was given authority over every tribe, people, language and nation. All inhabitants of the earth will worship the beast."

THE SECOND COMING

THE WORLD IS JUDGED BY A SAVIOR

In the Olivet Discourse (Matthew 24, Mark 13, and Luke 21), Jesus reveals "as a prophet" information detailing His return. It is most unusual and certainly noteworthy that He connects His return with the end of the world. This is another one of those strange coincidences, an eerie connection. Even during World War II, man could not destroy himself or his planet until the advent of nuclear weapons. Man can destroy this planet ten times over in this generation—that's a first.

I advise all to read each of these discourses and become familiar with Jesus as a prophet. There is a composite of divine information provided in them. Let it be said that Jesus is very specific as he answers the question the Jews ask. There is no mystery to His words so I'll let them speak for themselves. But for clarity's sake, I do have a few comments. (All verses in the following section are from Matthews 24.)

Remember who is asking the questions—the Jews! This is an important distinction to keep in mind lest we confuse ourselves. Christ is speaking "through" the Jews about the world in general with a great deal of the Scripture for just the Jews. For example, verses 15 through 22 are events in Jerusalem and probably all of Israel. Christ is warning them of a great distress to come like none other before.

It is amazing that I see other religions recognize Christ as a prophet more than Christian churches themselves. Islam is famous for declaring such; however, there is one problem—from their point of view, he was only a prophet. They downplay his virgin birth. Let us not do the same. Verses 23 through 28 warn about false Christs and false prophets. Heed His warning. The churches need to introduce Jesus as a prophet considering all we do see. I think a significant barrier to the churches is an unwillingness to preach Jesus's Jewish ancestry, and when they do, they treat the relationship as forever severed. But the Lord does indeed ponder the heart. Hear His prophetic message!

It is relatively sound to conclude that verses 5 through 31 represent the seven-year tribulation period. I can already "see" the world entering an agitated and distressful mind set. I forewarn all that such is going to literally increase to an almost uncontrollable feeling of desperation. As a world mass of unbelievers watch their world go through these prophetic changes, their reaction will be anger. Israel will eventually be considered the "problem." These will indeed be those terrible times. Only those anchored in truth will have discernment!

Verse 42 says "Watch therefore." We definitely are in a most challenging period, a generaton of transition. Churches are not considering the literal interpretation of the Bible and are blinding themselves by their symbolic approach. A literal God speaks literally. If we, in our stubbornness, refuse to change, let us remember the plight of Israel and let us remember them well.

They serve as an example in their failure to recognize Jesus when He first came. Therefore, we have even a lesser excuse. We see the signs, therefore let us receive the prophetic message which is the truth as God Himself has performed it, no matter the bitterness thereof. I know that truth is sweet to the receiver of the message but can be bitter to those whom I reveal it to.

And consider this: Concerning the seven letters addressing the seven churches in the Book of Revelations, Jesus judges the churches by their "works" but commands them to "repent." He forewarns each church of unique trials to come and then speaks to the individual who overcomes and what his reward will be. I believe that Christ is writing to religious people who are in the Lord's House but have been found in need of repentance at the time of the rapture, despite their "works." The just shall live by faith, and what is faith without hope? And what should be the hope of the Church? The apostles proclaim of His return, and so do I. The question is do you?

THE PARABLES OF HARVEST

THE PARABLE OF THE WHEAT and the tares is found in Matthew 13:24–30. Verse 30 reads, "Let both grow together until the harvest: and in the time of the harvest I will say to the reapers, Gather ye together first the tares and bind them in bundles to burn them: but gather the wheat into my barn." After the Jews asked the meaning of this parable, Jesus answers in verses 38 through 40—"The field is the world: the good seed are the children of the kingdom; but the tares are the children of the wicked one. The enemy that sowed them is the devil; the harvest is the end of the world; and the reapers are the angels. As therefore the tares are gathered and burned in the fire; so shall it be in the end of this world."

The parable of the sheep and the goats is found in Matthews 25:31–46. Verses 31–33 read, "When the Son of man shall come in his glory, and all the holy angels with him, then shall he sit upon the throne of his glory: And before Him shall be gathered all nations: and he shall separate them one from another, as a shepherd divideth his sheep from the goats: And he shall set the sheep on his right hand, but the goats on the left." Verse 46 concludes, "And these shall go away into everlasting punishment: but the righteous into life eternal."

Even after the battle of Armageddon, there will be survivors. Ezekiel 39:2 reveals that one-sixth will be left standing. It is clear that there will be men alive that must be judged. And those that are his sheep enter into the millennial kingdom of a thousand-year rule under Christ. These parables, which have often been treated as symbolic, have an unerring potential to be very literal as well. It is written in 2 Peter 3:9–10, "The Lord is not slack concerning his promise, as some men count slackness; but is lon-suffering toward us, not willing that any should perish, but that all should come to repentance. But the day of the Lord will come as a thief in the night; in which the heavens shall pass away with a great noise, and the elements shall melt with fervent heat, the earth also and the works that are therein shall be burned up."

God declares, "I am God, and there is none else; I am God, and there is none like me, declaring the end from the beginning, and from ancient times the things that are not yet done, saying, My counsel shall stand, and I will do all my pleasure'…yea, I have spoken it, I will also bring it to pass; I have purposed it, I will also do it" (Isaiah 46:9–11).

I "speak prophetically" these things, recognizing their potential and being moved and urged by the Holy Spirit to put forth what I have come to know for the benefit of others. For the great mystery is that man using his own "free will" will not see these things lest he feeds himself the Word of God. I, therefore, preach the gospel as John the Baptist in Matthews 3:2 says, "Repent ye: for the kingdom of heaven is at hand." Yes, the time of restitution is upon us, and a great day is not too far off. For it is written in 1 Corinthians 2:9 "Eye hath not seen, nor ear heard, neither have entered into the heart of man, the things which God hath prepared for them that love Him."

AND THIS IS THE FINAL INSTRUCTION

Our Lord speaks these words Matthew 10:32–33—"Whosoever therefore shall confess me before men, him will I confess also before my Father which is in heaven. But whosoever shall deny me before men, him will I also deny before my Father which is in heaven."

THE BATTLE OF ARMAGEDDON: HIS RETURN

EZEKIEL 38 AND 39 AND Revelation 19 speak very graphically, as if to leave no doubt of their unfulfillment...yet! God is indeed serious. I now understand His fury, His anger, and even His choice of words as He so clearly reveals. With God forgiving man of his many acts of unbelief time after time, He has allowed His reverence to be refused without quick retribution.

Again, the question of why becomes the key to the answer. His withholding of His wrath was necessary so that man would have a chance to demonstrate himself and all his faults and so that we may know the folly of free will outside of the Creator's will. I used to wonder why God considered Earth such a place of nobility with all the universe at His command. After much prayer, I received a very interesting answer to the question. In all the universe, this is the only planet where a creation of God is allowed to exercise the "I will." Yes, man has the unfortunate right to deny their own Creator and yet live. God has been passive for the benefit of those who are willing to elect Him amid all the deception. I do understand the reverence given to the Lord in Revelation 4:11 where it is written, "Thou art worthy, O Lord, to receive glory and honor and power: for thou hast created all things, and for thy pleasure they are and were created." It's as if He's proving something to the angelic realm and most certainly to His adversary...Satan. God's will is the best will.

Therefore, has not God been patient? Has He not given in, in order to get us out? There isn't one life form that asks of itself to be born before it is. Life is given regardless of the receiver, and it always desires to live no matter the odds. Let us understand God's wrath, considering the opportunities He gives. God asks all that Jesus could give and neither did yield. If God can ask so much of Jesus, what right can we dare say that God would never allow such a fate as the Book of Revelations reveals? We as Christians should always consider His tone. Read these Scriptures for they are indeed very plain. He will reach a point when he has had enough. And that point is drawing nearer day by day.

It is written, "Isaiah also crieth concerning Israel, Though the number of the children of Israel be as the sand of the sea, a remnant shall be saved: [and always will] For he will finish the work, and cut it short in righteousness: because a short work will the Lord make upon the earth" (Romans 9:27–28). Man is saved by grace, therefore, who can argue with the Lord's mercy when an end to sins must come? Man is condemned by his error of putting Christ on the cross. Yes, the Jews took the fall, but the unbelief of the Gentiles, except for a remnant also, proves their guilt as well. If the Gentiles refuse Christ after the resurrection has been demonstrated, whose error is the greater and whose judgment is more warranted? God does not condemn us for our errors, but we are condemned for our "lack of repentance." And so it has been for Israel; a national rejection requires a national repentance. The Lord has given man two thousand years of grace. I ask then, who can argue with the Lord's seven-year judgment?

God's primary purpose is to restore His glory and His honor before men. The Old Testament is filled with such a necessity. In addition, it is to give Christ the glory and honor as Judge and King. The Book of Daniel prophetically links Christ and His eternal kingdom. It acts to bridge Ezekiel and Revelations in a very dynamic way. One example is in Daniel 2:34 and 44–45. Notice the "stone" that is a reference to Jesus. Remember the question "Who is the stone that the builders rejected?" (See 1 Peter 2:4 and Matthews 21:24). Daniel 7 reveals more, as well as chapter 8 with the "Prince of Princes." This all reveals Jesus Himself destroying the Beast and his Ten-Horned Kingdom.

Concluding on the Prophetic Word

Much has been said, and personally I am exhausted from the physical time and energy that has been required of me. I have indeed been moved by the Spirit to put forth what must be heard. I know that He has chosen others who have chosen to receive, but even so, it is irrational to think that many will be able to proclaim it as I have written it. I know the great burden I had to overcome and the sacrifice it took to be worthy to receive such divine messages. Everyone has a Bible, and still they do not see. God has always used a minimum and achieved the maximum, further showing His power. No man is beyond Him!

There is a vicious cycle of events that are soon to occur. I hope you are blessed by the knowledge received, that your faith is charged, that your soul is stirred, and that your spirit is fed. Let it be said that my Creator is also yours; there is no preference, but there is accountability. And there are the promises. Little has been said about the promises, but much has been demonstrated in the person of Christ Himself. Are we not waiting for Him yet? Does His Word live to this very day two thousand years later? Moses himself now knows why he had to wait for the Promised Land. The world has expanded like no man knew it could but God Himself. God has literally fulfilled His Words in Revelation 5:9—"And they sung a new song, saying, 'Thou art worthy to take the book, and to open the seals thereof: for thou wast slain and hast redeemed us to God by the blood out of every kindred, and tongue, and people, and nation.'"

Little did Moses know what God meant when he told Abraham that he would be the father of many nations. God has performed a work of art. And yes, because of such a close relationship to God Himself, Israel has been blinded by the work of the Lord, however, of their own choosing. I see a world about to make the same error against Israel as Israel made against their Messiah for the Gentiles have blinded themselves. Yes, neither is the better as God has concluded that none is righteous, no, not one. And to all those proud men, God is set to prove them in their ways.

The subtleness of the Lord is stunning when you really consider all things. So consider all things I have written. Let us desire to know our Creator as a child yearns for his mother's presence. It is the one passion we all should seek out, and it requires faith. Feed your spirit, for man indeed does not live by bread alone but by every Word of the Living God.

Herein, I conclude this journey with the Word of the Lord. "For the wrath of God is revealed from heaven against all ungodliness and unrighteousness of men, who hold the truth in unrighteousness. Because that which may be known of God is manifest in them. For the invisible things of him from the creation of the world are clearly seen, being understood by the things that are made, even His eternal power and Godhead; so that they are without excuse" (Romans 1:18–20).

THE PROMISES AND THE CROWNS

IT IS WRITTEN IN 1 Corinthians 15:54–55, "So when this corruptible shall have put on incorruption, and this mortal shall have put on immortality, then shall be brought to pass the saying that is written, Death is swallowed up in victory. O death, where is thy sting? O grave, where is thy victory?" Let it be said that there is none cause greater than eternal life. Men and women will join armies and die for their country. Young kids join gangs and are willing to put their life on the line to be welcomed, and yet all that is promised is a medal and a flower on a grave. Man cannot give to himself anything more. Many people die for a cause every day. The world crowns its heroes constantly, whether they are athletes, politicians, soldiers, policemen, etc. Crowning isn't anything new, and receiving rewards is a natural part of man's achievements and recognition. God offers promises as well, and I know they will be performed at the appointed time. Let us know the prize, for the Lord has promised we shall receive it:

- The Crown of Life—This crown is promised to all those who have withstood the tribulations and martyrdom for Christ. Revelations 2:10 states, "Be thou faithful until death, and I will give you a crown of life."
- The Crown of Glory—Those who have served Jesus Christ in the role of elders and pastors will receive such. 1 Peter 5:14 states, "The elders which are among you...shall receive a crown of glory that fadeth not away."
- The Crown of Rejoicing—Those who have won others to faith in Jesus Christ as their Savior will receive this crown. 1 Thessalonians 2:19 states, "For what is our hope, or joy, or crown of rejoicing? Are not even ye in the presence of our Lord Jesus Christ at his coming?"
- The Crown of Righteousness—This crown is given to all Christians that long for the return of Christ. 2 Timothy 4:8 states, "There is laid up for me the crown of righteousness, which the

Lord, the righteous judge, shall give me at that day, and not to me only, but unto all them also that love his appearing."

- The Incorruptible Crown—This is a crown of purity for the victors in the daily spiritual struggle which we wage in our life. 1 Corinthians 9:25 (NKJV) reads, "And everyone who competes for the prize is temperate in all things. Now they do it to obtain a perishable crown, but we for an imperishable crown."

"For our citizenship is in heaven, from which we also eagerly await for the Savior, the Lord Jesus Christ: Who will transform our lowly body that it may be conformed to His glorious body, according to the working by which He is able even to subdue all things to Himself" (Philippians 3:20–21 NKJV)

Our Savior, the Christ, concludes, "I, Jesus, have sent my angel to give you a testimony for the churches. I am the Root and the Offspring of David, and the bright Morning Star. The Spirit and the bride say, 'Come!' And let the one who hears say, Come!' Let the one who is thirsty come; and let the one who wishes take the free gift of the water of life" (Revelation 22:16–17 NIV).

INSPIRED WRITINGS

I AM AFTER THEE, OH LORD

My Lord and My God

Hear my cry and know my praise… For I am after thee.

For I have searched the low places… Yea, the hidden places
have I sought thee out.

In my soul do I climb to the peak of the highest mountain

That I may Find the God of my salvation

Am I not lifted up by thy Grace

And made to sing by thine abundant mercies?

I am after thee, Oh Lord.

And in my flesh I cannot find thee.

But only in my spirit shall you be found.

I travel the path of the bumblebee, seeking thee,

Seeming to have no direct path…

Yet only is my destination made sure by your leading hand.

And so I am found by thee, and my path do become straight.

I am made a servant of the Lord

And a friend unto Jesus, the Rock of my salvation.

By thy Spirit am I broken, but by thy Spirit Was I strengthened.

Think well of me, Oh Lord,

That I might not be made to battle the Wind of the Spirit

For I do seek to rest as thou giveth Man in his beginning.

In me there is a secret storm calmed only by a still, small voice.

Yes, even a silent thunder

For my Lord will know the praise that dwells in me.

For it is a certainty that I shall not be silenced.

And let not even sin encroach upon me

For will not my spirit hide from thee.

Thou I may stumble, the power of thy salvation will be holding me up.

And I shall forever repent for only thee is forever righteous.

Only thee is forever without sin, my Lord Jesus.

Therefore, I rest my case under Thy cross

And seek no more for my peace… It is found!

For it is thy Spirit that has determined that it should be found.

Thou has heard my cry, and my voice has been heard.

Therefore, thou shall forever hear my praise

For thy sacrifice has cleansed me

And thou salvation has made me whole.

I am after thee, Oh Lord, for thou is a secret God,

And you search for seekers after you and you only.

Blessed are those who are after the Lord

And look for Him daily in the way of goings… Amen.

CLOSING THOUGHTS: A "BACK-TO-BASICS" GOSPEL

I HOPE YOU ENJOYED THE reading of this collection of writings. To me, it was an experience to be revealed even though such a "telling" was not my initial purpose or desire. I declare that God moved me in a way that He must be spoken of, and so I ultimately have done just that. It is indeed bold to declare oneself a prophet, but instead I think of myself as a minister of God's Prophetic Word. I do believe God is restoring this ministry in preparation of Christ's return. The true prophet will do as the Scripture requires in 1 Corinthians 14:3—"But he that prophesieth speaketh unto men to edification, exhortation, and to comfort." I hope this material produces the fruit of faith and joy.

I have shared these writings with individuals many times and have seen how people have been blessed by them. All I desire is for people to see what I see. These writings hopefully should educate as well as forewarn because there is a refresher to the Gospel coming that will shake all our comfort zones. Christ will be the centerpiece as always, but according to the Word, Israel is His purpose for returning, and we must be prepared to say "Amen and Amen!" Salvation will be Israel's at last, and my hope is we don't reject this truth as written in the Word as Israel rejected His first coming, which was in the Word. Sad to say, despite the forewarnings, wisdom dictates many will reject this reality to their own hurt, for it is already written.

Satan is revealing his mastery of making man not see what he should be able to see. So it was in the Garden of Eden, so it was two thousand years ago when Israel failed and put Christ on the cross, and so it is even now as the Gentile world (including those un-born-again, unaware, unbelieving church folk) is being led to put Israel on the cross. Could God be testing us in much the same way as Israel was tested? And are we and even the churches above being tested? I certainly think not! Oh, the wisdom of the Lord! Hindu, Buddhism, Islam, Atheism, witchcraft, and every other false religion is about to be cast down. This is why the battle of Armageddon is on the borders of Israel. God is set to demonstrate one thing and one thing only, and that is—what truth is and where it sits! Now it comes down to He that overcome, not a denominational preference, but a realization of His Word and that it is heard.

If you notice, this is not religion, but belief in His Word by a born-again experience with a personal relationship with Christ which is far more than just church, a distinction that needs to be acknowledged more and more with each passing day. May this book help the process of encouraging you to look at God's Word with a fresh anointing.

My heart cries out constantly for the world to hear these things, but they are so consumed. But every now and then, God sends me someone who does *hear*, and that makes this effort worth every bit of my time. And so I press on with this New Gospel, which is bridging Israel and the Church into one holy entity in preparation of the kingdom to come, led by Christ, "Lord of Lord and King of Kings." Such is a Back-to-Basics gospel!

At times my writings may have appeared chaotic as I sought to merge and republish the message. However, my goal and motive has always been to refresh or liven up the hope that is in our Savior Jesus Christ. I desire an evangelistic voice that I hope gives birth to a revival. The end times is also about new times. The Book of Revelations announces the coming Kingdom of Christ when death is no more and it loses it sting forever among men.

The seven letters, as they are named in the book, were written before any of the inspirational writings scattered throughout the letters. Both sets of writings give detailed accounts of prophetic events that are stated in Scripture and proclaimed to be revealed in an *inspired* setting. I believe the seven letters exercise the gift of prophecy written in a more formal and conventional manner. They have supporting Scripture and fully grasp the complexities and paradoxes that can exist when studying biblical prophecy. It is recommended reading regardless of denominational setting or national/ racial heritage.

And so it is written in Ephesians 2:5–8 (NIV), "It is by grace you have been saved. And God has raised us up with Christ and seated us with him in the heavenly realms in Christ Jesus, in order that in the coming ages he might show the incomparable riches of his grace, expressed in his kindness to us in Christ Jesus. For it is by grace you have been saved through faith—and this is not from yourselves, it is the gift of God."

A "BACK-TO-BASICS" GOSPEL

THE GOSPEL'S OBJECTIVE IS "A prophetic ministry to assure us of the purpose of Jesus Christ." The four founding principles are:

1. Let us know that the perfect will of God is that we might have a "saving" knowledge in Jesus Christ. Key founding scripture: John 15.

2. Let us know that the purpose and the power of prophecy is that we might have a "more sure word" from God the Father. Key founding scripture: 2 Peter 1:16–21.

3. Let us desire a fuller measure of the Holy Spirit by offering a fuller measure of repentance so that we might receive the gifts of the Holy Spirit and manifest the fruit of His presence. Key founding scripture: Acts 2:37–38 and Galatians 5:22–23.

4. May the blessed hope of the church yet be the earnest expectation of the second coming of Jesus Christ "for we which are alive and remain." Key founding scripture: 1 Thessalonians 4:13–18.

FOUNDING FRUIT OF THIS GOSPEL MINISTRY AND THE OVERSEER POSITION

- Founding fruit—*Seven Letters Detailing the Prophetic Framework of the Return of Christ* by Gregory Booker
- Overseer name—Gregory A. Booker
- Title—Minister of the Prophetic Word (1 Corinthians 14:3)
- Vehicle—Evangelism (Ephesians 4:11)
- Gifts of the Holy Spirit manifested for the perfecting of the saints
- 1 Corinthians 12:1–11 "And these are the gifts the Lord giveth me"—Word of knowledge…word of wisdom…discerning of spirits, culminating into the operation of…the gift of prophecy
- Final statement—"I submit myself to the calling of the Lord for the purpose of the churches that they might be edified, exhorted, and yet comforted as we the bride are made ready for the return of our Lord the Christ."
- Standard of conduct—"Present your bodies a living sacrifice" (Romans 12)
- The opponent—"Let us not be deceived, for what should be obvious… obviously is not! Such is the work of the adversary."
- Our armor—"Stand…loins girt about with truth. Breastplate of righteousness. Feet prepared for peace. Shield of faith. Helmet of salvation…and the Word as the sword!" (Ephesians 6)
- Motto—"Discretion shall preserve thee, understanding shall keep thee" (Proverbs 2:11)

JUSTIFICATION FOR A "BACK-TO-BASICS" GOSPEL

I DID NOT PLAN TO be what I now have become. I simply had a curiosity about prophecy and thereby sought out a better understanding of Jesus Christ, who I admittedly knew little about. That search began in November 1989 after reading Hal Lindsey's book titled *The Late Great Planet Earth*. That book focused on fulfilled and unfulfilled prophecy. It highlighted the nation of Israel and Christ's kinship to that nation. So, I continued down this path, studying a variety of books by a variety of writers on this subject.

After a period of saturation, I was suddenly directed by a voice in my conscious which said commandingly, "Now write what you have come to know." And so I immediately sat down and wrote my first letter dated May 16, 1990, and concluded with the seventh letter written in July 1991. Throughout this writing period, I shared the letters with anyone who had an ear to hear. I specifically sought out ministers for their critical review that they might assess their scriptural soundness and perhaps benefit themselves and their congregation, if such information was unknown to them. This was done first out of respect for their position in the Lord's House.

On this day in December 1992, I have shared the first three letters with over two-hundred-and-fifty people of which approximately thirty-five were ministers, and approximately seventy people have been given all seven letters. While I am elated that not one minister has rebuked me for correction, I am saddened that neither have they supported the conclusion that the letters do reveal. It is peculiar that the "Hope" that I have yet to deliver has caused many of the flock to be moved but not the shepherds. I am therefore disappointed with the ministers lack of response. Their silence (with the exception of a few) disturbs me concerning righteousness for did not Jesus say, "Let him who is without sin cast the first stone" and none did for they all left in silence. Silence has its own thunder!

It is for this reason that I have been moved to initiate a "Back-to-Basics" gospel. Truly, I do not desire my own church but to preach to and in the churches that already are as an evangelist. There are more than enough churches with empty pews. Most people indicate to me that their churches are without true fellowship among one another. They are either too money oriented, too pride based, too pretentious, or simply too unscriptural. Let, therefore, this ministry seek to give answers to those who dare to have questions in these most perplexing times.

This ministry is a reactive one. I conclude that many have forgotten their first love (Jesus) that they have little or no hope in His return, and without hope one must ask then, "Where is their faith?" Let me say that it is not so important that what I have written is right, but what is most important is that we who are called Christians must always believe and yet desire the earnest expectation of Jesus Christ. It is the proof of our belief in the resurrection, and anything less than that shall prevent us from overcoming doubt which is the enemy to faith.

This ministry will seek to provide an avenue for those saints who simply desire to know what I feel the Holy Spirit has given us to know and me ultimately to write down for the benefit of others. It is unique, and it is my desire to draw people into this ministry for the purpose of sending them back to their home churches to spread the good news of this gospel. I have tried the front door of the minister's office, shall we now enter the back door by way of the congregation?

For the present, let us call this an "undercover" ministry having no physical location but with the exception of your body, also known as the temple of God for those who worship the Christ. Scripture desires we all might prophesy but not that we must all be prophets, for it is the Lord that giveth! Let our main objective be this—To use prophecy for the purpose of proving our belief and making known our hope so that in that day we might be found worthy and blameless due to our faith. Therefore, desirable unto the Lord, we shall be "caught up" by our Lord, removing us from that great day of evil that is indeed approaching upon this generation. And what is the purpose of this evil? It is so that Israel shall be delivered from a world of unbelief, and conclusively, God shall demonstrate Himself and the glory that is in His Son the Christ. And thus, truth shall be revealed and proven.

I CLOSE WITH AN OUTPOURING

OH MY GOD, GREAT IS thy countenance. For I knew not myself and my sins till I knew Thee and thy righteousness. Yes, one has revealed the other. Thy grace is known unto me and may it be known to all. I am convicted by thy work, Lord Jesus who made Himself a little lower, that I might know my Creator and be saved by His salvation. He is our consolation determined not to be absent from us.

But we must accept Him by acknowledging ourselves for what we are. I strike down the pride which blinds me to His purpose. Has He not proven Himself? I seek not to earn my salvation but to speak it and speak it clear and bold, to let it be known as He would have it. Am I a testimony to His cause? Do I seek for myself? For no price or purchase I do give freely that which has been freely given to me by the grace of God who desires that we know these things at His urging. The Spirit has spoken and I have heard. The Spirit has directed and I did write. Therefore, wash in the blood of Jesus who was and is a living sacrifice for all the world that they all might be saved. For all do come short of the glory of God, and it is His holiness that we should desire to stand in. Yes, in His footprints doth the Spirit of Truth require of us that we may be sealed now and forever more. And I know I have been held and reserved for this cause that a few more may be brought in by the hearing of this gospel and that the truth may be known before His hand of judgment is determined. It is by His grace that I have received of it.

Therefore, I must stand and yet must I speak what has been written as it has been written. I fear the Lord above all and love Jesus who first loved us. I am accountable, but am I not also strengthened? I do stand up because now I *can* stand up! On this day, may the Lord use me mightily as He has indeed prepared me to stand before the congregation that I might proclaim the things to come. Called to reveal and to forewarn, am I not also called to cry? For by my revealing, I must forewarn, and by the silence, I do cry. Nevertheless, I stand firm that the True God shall demonstrate Himself for the purpose of His Son that He will be glorified in that day. In the name of Jesus the Christ I do pray. Amen and Amen!

Gregory A. Booker

A NOTE OF THANKS

I WOULD LIKE TO GIVE my personal thanks to all those who have taken their precious time to read my letters. I had no idea that I would write, and I certainly had no idea I could be so blessed to write so convincingly as many of my readers have acknowledged. Let it be said that your praises are well received and have indeed been a part of my continued inspiration. I am an imperfect vehicle used by a perfect vehicle, the Holy Spirit. I am convinced of His presence, and I hope that others are too by the reading of my words. If Jehovah's Witnesses, Mormons, New Age, and countless others can so openly preach things that are not of the Bible, why can't I try just as hard to preach the Bible? Have I not defined the truth? I do pray to minimize my opinions to maximize the Spirit's. So therefore, how can I glory in my own writings? Let it be said that I do not, for the message is His, and I am but a messenger called to reveal and to forewarn based on faith. Since the beginning of time, has it not always been faith and faith alone? I have been blessed to see the results of faith, and so I share so that all may see it also as clear as the blue skies and as sure as the Bible in your hand.

When I wrote my first letter titled "The Necessity of the Return of God's Chosen People," I had no intentions of writing another and another, etc. But it is clear that the Holy Spirit had other ideas. And so I was compelled to write as it is written in 1 Corinthians 9:16, "For thou I preach the gospel, I have nothing to glory of: for necessity is laid upon me; yea, woe is unto me, if I preach not the gospel."

It is clear to me that these letters are written with the intent to be spoken. They are in essence "preaching letters." The beauty in them is their clarity. This allows the reader to address them to others based on faith alone. God seems to be excusing a lack of knowledge, but He will never excuse lack of faith. This is the perplexing situation of the tribulation saints as our Lord prepares for Israel's promised redemption.

Oh, let us hear the voice of the Lord as He restores His people!

Yes, let us acknowledge the Spirit of Truth, call for justice!

Indeed, has He not elected Israel for our sake?

Prepare ye the way

Our Lord does speak and I have heard His tone

And I have heard His command!

As it is written in Isaiah 62:6 and 7

"I have set watchmen upon thy walls, O Jerusalem, which shall never hold their peace day nor night: ye that make mention of the Lord, Keep not silence. And give Him no rest, till He establish, and till he make Jerusalem a praise in the earth."

Indeed, I do watch and cannot keep silent.

Amen!!!

Gregory A. Booker

ACKNOWLEDGMENTS

AND FINALLY GIVING CREDIT WHERE credit is due, I acknowledge to those a listing of books which have all aided me in my search for truth. Though my learning has not been through an accredited school of ministry, let it be known that I needed the efforts of those who did dedicate themselves through the collegiate process. Let us take advantage of the reading material available, and may the listing provided give you a running start. Thanks be to the writers, thanks indeed!

The Kingdoms of the Lord by David F. Payne

The Day Jerusalem Burned by unknown

The History of the Jews by unknown

The Late Great Planet Earth by Hal Lindsey

Satan is Alive and Well by Hal Lindsey

The Return by Michael Evans

The Rapture by Hal Lindsey

Silence is Thunder by Joel Goldsmith

Flying Saucers and The Bible by Barry H. Downing

The Day of the Holocaust by Hal Lindsey

Holy Places: "Jews, Christians, and Islam" by Christopher Hollis

Armageddon: Appointment with Destiny by Grant Jeffrey

Troubling Biblical Waters by Hope Cain Felder

Combat Faith by Hal Lindsey

Till Armageddon by Billy Graham

Heaven…The Last Frontier by Grant Jeffrey

Angels on Commission by Billy Graham

Jesus, An Interview Across Time by Andy G. Hodges, MD

War in the Heavenlies by Benny Hinn

The Gifts of the Spirit by J. W. MacGorman

And, of course, the *Thompson Chain Reference Bible*, 4th Edition, and *The Dake's Annotated Reference Bible*.

A special thanks to the writers of faith who gave me the curiosity to look into the Word of yesterday to see the hope of our tomorrows.